GOD'S LAST MESSAGE

CHRIST OUR RIGHTEOUSNESS

NO FICTION. JUST FACTS.

I
YOU SHALL HAVE NO OTHER GODS BEFORE ME.

II
YOU SHALL NOT MAKE FOR YOURSELF A CARVED IMAGE, ANY LIKENESS OF ANYTHING THAT IS IN HEAVEN ABOVE, OR THAT IS IN THE EARTH BENEATH, OR THAT IS IN THE WATER UNDER THE EARTH; YOU SHALL NOT BOW DOWN TO THEM NOR SERVE THEM. FOR I, THE LORD YOUR GOD, AM A JEALOUS GOD, VISITING THE INIQUITY OF THE FATHERS UPON THE CHILDREN TO THE THIRD AND FOURTH GENERATIONS OF THOSE WHO HATE ME, BUT SHOWING MERCY TO THOUSANDS, TO THOSE WHO LOVE ME AND KEEP MY COMMANDMENTS.

III
YOU SHALL NOT TAKE THE NAME OF THE LORD YOUR GOD IN VAIN, FOR THE LORD WILL NOT HOLD HIM GUILTLESS WHO TAKES HIS NAME IN VAIN.

IV
REMEMBER THE SABBATH DAY, TO KEEP IT HOLY. SIX DAYS YOU SHALL LABOR AND DO ALL YOUR WORK, BUT THE SEVENTH DAY IS THE SABBATH OF THE LORD YOUR GOD. IN IT YOU SHALL DO NO WORK: YOU, NOR YOUR SON, NOR YOUR DAUGHTER, NOR YOUR MALE SERVANT, NOR YOUR FEMALE SERVANT, NOR YOUR CATTLE, NOR YOUR STRANGER WHO IS WITHIN YOUR GATES. FOR IN SIX DAYS THE LORD MADE THE HEAVENS AND THE EARTH, THE SEA, AND ALL THAT IS IN THEM, AND RESTED THE SEVENTH DAY. THEREFORE THE LORD BLESSED THE SABBATH DAY AND HALLOWED IT.

V
HONOR YOUR FATHER AND YOUR MOTHER, THAT YOUR DAYS MAY BE LONG UPON THE LAND WHICH THE LORD YOUR GOD IS GIVING YOU.

VI
YOU SHALL NOT MURDER.

VII
YOU SHALL NOT COMMIT ADULTERY.

VIII
YOU SHALL NOT STEAL.

IX
YOU SHALL NOT BEAR FALSE WITNESS AGAINST YOUR NEIGHBOR.

X
YOU SHALL NOT COVET YOUR NEIGHBOR'S HOUSE; YOU SHALL NOT COVET YOUR NEIGHBOR'S WIFE, NOR HIS MALE SERVANT, NOR HIS FEMALE SERVANT, NOR HIS OX, NOR HIS DONKEY, NOR ANYTHING THAT IS YOUR NEIGHBOR'S.

STEVE WOHLBERG

Pacific Press®
Publishing Association

Nampa, Idaho | Oshawa, Ontario, Canada
www.pacificpress.com

Cover design by Charles Lawson, White Horse Media
Cover resources from Charles Lawson
Inside design by Kristin Hansen-Mellish

Unless otherwise marked, Scripture quotations are taken from the New King James Version®. Copyright © 1982 by Thomas Nelson, Inc. Used by permission. All rights reserved.

The author assumes full responsibility for the accuracy of all facts and quotations as cited in this book.

You can obtain additional copies of this book by calling toll-free 1-800-765-6955 or by visiting http://www.adventistbookcenter.com.

ISBN 13: 978-0-8163-4519-9
ISBN 10: 0-8163-4519-8

13 14 15 16 17 • 5 4 3 2 1

Dedicated to the Son of God,
who saves me by His marvelous grace!

Special thanks to Clinton Wahlen.
Your faithful research on the message of Ellet J. Waggoner about "Christ Our Righteousness" in the year 1888 was extremely helpful.

CONTENTS

FOREWORD

The Bible says that Christ in you is the hope of glory (see Colossians 1:27). When one takes a comprehensive overview of the Scriptures, it becomes very clear that Jesus Christ should be all and in all. Jesus stated, "You search the Scriptures, for in them you think you have eternal life; and these are they which testify of Me" (John 5:39). From the Creation to the giving of the Law, to the Guide in the wilderness, to the first Advent, and all the way down to the New Earth, Christ has been active in humanity's behalf. Indeed, the whole Bible testifies of Him.

All thinking people, and most definitely all committed Christians, recognize that we are near the end of time. Soon Jesus will come! Satan knows this and is doing his utmost to keep mankind deluded, deceived, occupied, and entranced until probation closes (see Revelation 22:11). We must get ready now. As the Scriptures declare in Peter's great sermon upholding Christ, "Nor is there salvation in any other, for there is no other name under heaven given among men by which we must be saved" (Acts 4:12).

The bottom line is simple. We must come to Christ!

Studies I have done in doing research for my book, *Even at the Door,* convinced me that the second coming of Christ is literally at the door. I have presented this message at camp meetings, ministers' meetings, and in seminars all across the United States and Canada. During one of my appointments I had what I consider to be a providential meeting with another presenter, Pastor Steve Wohlberg. His presentations on the righteousness of Christ were the most balanced and practical I had ever heard. I encouraged Steve to put the material he presented into book form so it could have wide circulation. In this book, *God's Last Message: Christ Our Righteousness,* he has done so. As you read it, I trust you will be pleased with his positive approach and simple, easy-to-understand presentation.

Much of what we receive in the mail today is what I consider to be junk mail—mail order catalogs, business offers, advertisements, encouragements to get involved in sweepstakes in which I "may already be a winner." Most of this stuff, along with much of what is on TV today, is simply rubbish—trash.

There are, however, some things that deserve a portion of our precious time, things that have significance and life-changing value, things to occupy one's mind that could have eternal consequences. In the overall scheme of things it doesn't really matter who wins the World Series or whether or not there is even another World Series. What matters most is eternal life. Considering the big picture, it is the only thing that matters. The Bible, God's Word, is the road map that will see us through the times ahead and lead us into the Kingdom of Glory. We all need to spend more time reading it and other materials like "the spirit of prophecy" (see Revelation 19:10) that will direct us back to God's Word.

I believe that Steve Wohlberg's book is well worth reading. I have been blessed and encouraged by his presentations on this marvelous subject.

My prayer is that you will be too.

G. Edward Reid, author, *Even at the Door,* former stewardship director of the North American Division of Seventh-day Adventists

INTRODUCTION

The life-saving episode happened in October of 2008, during the time of the Second Congo War (also known as the Great War in Africa), which was the deadliest war in modern African history. More than 5.4 million people perished.

Sixteen-year-old "J" (we don't know his full name) was lucky. Or was it divine providence in his behalf? Unexpectedly, a fierce hippopotamus sank its teeth into the boy's left arm, placing his life in immediate jeopardy. An emergency partial amputation inches below his shoulder offered temporary relief, but when a severe infection developed in the left shoulder, hope faded fast.

In a few days, J would join the dead.

Dr. David Nott, an on-site British surgeon doing volunteer work for Doctors Without Borders, refused to give up. But he knew he needed help from afar. Trying his best to remain calm, Dr. Nott quickly phoned his surgical colleague in England, Professor Meirino Thomas, a consultant at the Royal Marsden Hospital in London, seeking expert advice.

No answer. Dr. Nott tried email. Again, no answer.

As a last resort, Dr. Nott sent Dr. Thomas a text message from his cell phone. Shortly thereafter, Dr. Nott's phone beeped back. Hurray! It was a message from Dr. Thomas, who was away on vacation at the time. A newspaper headline later read, "Text Messages Guide Life-Saving Amputation in Africa."[1]

Dr. Thomas's text messages contained detailed instructions about how to amputate the infected shoulder. With only a scalpel, forceps, minimal anesthesia, and a pint of blood, Dr. Nott began the emergency procedure and successfully removed J's entire left shoulder. The crisis was over. Onlookers were thrilled!

Again, this incident occurred during a terrible time of war.

A vicious beast had attacked a young teenager.

Text messages mercifully sent from halfway around the world by a caring physician saved the boy's life.

Dear reader, whether you realize it or not, we are participants in the final stages of the greatest war of all, the Great Controversy between Jesus Christ, the Prince of Life, and a heavenly angel formerly named Lucifer, who rebelled against His rightful authority (see Isaiah 14:12–14 and Revelation 12:7–9). The stakes are enormous. The casualties are global. The issues are life and death. As we approach the climax of this fierce conflict, the Holy Bible warns, "Woe to the inhabitants of the earth and the sea! For the devil has come down to you, having great wrath, because he knows that he has a short time" (Revelation 12:12).

According to this verse, Lucifer is furious because he realizes his days are numbered. He knows that "the lake of fire and brimstone" (Revelation 20:10) awaits him and his infernal forces. Just as a deadly African creature attacked J, even so are wicked satanic agencies constantly harassing, tempting, and attacking us. Through yielding to demonic trickery, we've all been "foolish, disobedient, [and] deceived" (Titus 3:3) at least once in our lives. More like thousands. To make matters worse, the Bible's last book informs us that "the hour of [God's] judgment has come" (Revelation 14:7). Soon "each of us shall give account of himself to God" (Romans 14:12).

For the majority, it won't be pretty.

Indeed, the entire human family is in trouble. If we are to survive Armageddon and reach a holy heaven, we desperately need help from afar, just as Dr. Nott needed emergency guidance from faraway England. But, ah, there is good news! Just as Professor Thomas responded in a pinch by sending life-giving text messages, even so has God Almighty mercifully sent *a special end-time message* to aid humanity during planet Earth's closing crisis hour.

If you search diligently, you will discover that the book of Revelation calls that special message *the third angel's message* (see Revelation 14:9–12). This message's targeted purpose is to prepare men, women, and children for the glorious return of Jesus Christ.

Notice carefully: "Then *a third angel* followed them, saying with a loud voice . . ." (Revelation 14:9; emphasis added).

The third angel's call concludes with: "Here is the patience of the saints; here are those who keep the commandments of God and the faith of Jesus" (verse 12).

Then John wrote: "Then I looked, and behold, a white cloud, and on the cloud sat One like the Son of Man, having on His head a golden crown, and in His hand a sharp sickle" (Revelation 14:14).

According to this inspired sequence, the third angel's message results in the development of a final, apocalyptic group of "saints" who literally "keep the commandments of God" (verse 12), meaning the Ten Commandments, right before Jesus Christ returns on "a white cloud" (verse 14) to reap the harvest of the earth. Thus Jesus is coming to rescue Ten Commandment–*keepers,* not Ten Commandment–*breakers.*

How is this possible? How can any group of sinners (which is what we all are by nature) genuinely obey God's Law? Especially when Paul informs us that "all have sinned and fall short of the glory of God" (Romans 3:23)? The answer is—and it is the purpose of this book to explore this truth—*through the gift of Jesus Christ's spotless righteousness.*

An ancient Old Testament prophecy predicted that someday the Bethlehem Baby would be known by a special name, "THE LORD OUR RIGHTEOUSNESS" (Jeremiah 23:6).

That ancient prophecy is being fulfilled today.

Now here's some unusual, surprising information, which will be thoroughly explained in the following pages. Although few Christians know anything about it, more than a hundred years ago, God Almighty raised up two young ministers—who were members of the controversial Seventh-day Adventist Church—and taught them *from the Bible* the third angel's message centered in the righteousness of Jesus Christ. Their names were Alonzo T. Jones and Ellet J. Waggoner. In October of the year 1888, an Adventist General Conference Session for pastors and leaders took place in the city of Minneapolis, Minnesota, and Jones and Waggoner stepped off a train as delegates from California. At that meeting, those two Californians preached and lifted up Jesus Christ, exalted His cross, and forcibly presented the free gift of His righteousness to their hearers, "not with persuasive words of human wisdom, but in demonstration of the Spirit and of power" (1 Corinthians 2:4).

Sitting in the audience was a short, elderly woman named Ellen G. White, who, even to this day, has maintained the notable distinction of being the most translated American nonfiction author who has ever lived. With more than forty books to her credit translated into more than 140 languages, the late Walter Martin described her as "one of the most fascinating and controversial personages ever to appear upon the horizon of religious history."[2] Not only was Mrs. White one of the pioneers of the Seventh-day Adventist Church (officially organized in 1863), but also she has for more than a hundred years been regarded by millions around the world as having a special gift which the New Testament labels "the spirit of prophecy" (see Revelation 19:10; Acts 2:17; 21:8). Those who carefully read her books recognize that her writings agree with Scripture.

In 1888, *The Minneapolis Journal* ran a news story about the Adventist conference that had convened in its city. Reporting on one of the sessions, the *Journal* declared:

> A little woman who was sitting in a large rocking chair on the right hand side arose and addressed the meetings. She spoke in slow, distinct and impressive tones. Every word she uttered seemed to make an

impression. . . . The speaker was no less a person than the renowned Sister Ellen G. White, one of the most remarkable women in the world today. Mrs. White is now 61 years old, but her hair is just tinged with gray. . . . Mrs. White has fame not only as a speaker on temperance and religious topics, but she is a voluminous writer. She has written a *Life of Christ, Sketches of the Life of Paul,* and a kind of history of Christianity which she has called the *Conflict of Christ and Satan.* But the most remarkable product of her pen is a series of volumes called *Testimonies.* These contain a history of her visions in which she received warnings and admonitions for the benefit of the "latter church." She is supposed to have "special light" in regard to the signs that were to indicate the coming of the last days that precede the end of the world.[3]

After hearing both Jones and Waggoner speak amidst beautifully colored autumn leaves blowing briskly throughout Minneapolis, Mrs. White later enthusiastically reported:

The Lord in His great mercy sent a most precious message to His people through Elders Waggoner and Jones. This message was to bring more prominently before the world the uplifted Saviour, the sacrifice for the sins of the whole world. It presented justification through faith in the Surety; it invited the people to receive the righteousness of Christ, which is made manifest in obedience to all the commandments of God. Many had lost sight of Jesus. They needed to have their eyes directed to His divine person, His merits, and His changeless love for the human family. All power is given into His hands, that He may dispense rich gifts unto men, imparting the priceless gift of His own righteousness to the helpless human agent. This is the message that God commanded to be given to the world. It is the third angel's message, which is to be proclaimed with a loud voice, and attended with the outpouring of His Spirit in a large measure.[4]

I realize this information may be new to many of my readers, and if you belong to a Christian denomination besides Seventh-day Adventism you may be tempted to set this book aside forever. If so, I beg of you, please, stick with me, at least for a while. If you do, I promise that within the following pages you will not only discover life-changing *biblical facts* about Heaven's eternal moral law, the Ten Commandments, "written with the finger of God" (Exodus 31:18), but also the greatest treasure Heaven has ever offered to sinful mortals, the "white garments" (Revelation 3:18) of Jesus Christ's own righteousness, which He longs to impart to each of us before it's too late.

The biblical message that Jesus Christ is "THE LORD OUR RIGH-
TEOUSNESS" (Jeremiah 23:6) is God Almighty's life-saving message to humanity from afar. In these closing hours of the Great War, the Lord Himself
has sent it. As an additional aid, He has also sent His Holy Spirit to help us
locate that message in the books of Romans, Galatians, and Revelation.

Professor Meirino Thomas's emergency text message to Dr. Nott in Africa
saved a boy's life.

God's message will save our souls.

It's center is not J but JESUS.

Enjoy the journey.

---

1. K. C. Jones, "Text Messages Guide Life-Saving Amputation In Africa,"
Information Week, Dec. 4, 2008, http://www.informationweek.com/mobility/
messaging/text-messages-guide-life-saving-amputati/212202008.

2. Walter Martin, *The Kingdom of the Cults* (Minneapolis: Bethany, 1965),
379.

3. *The Minneapolis Journal,* October 20, 1888.

4. Ellen G. White, *Testimonies to Ministers and Gospel Workers* (Mountain
View, CA: Pacific Press® Publishing Association, 1923), 91, 92; emphasis added.

CHAPTER ONE

A BURST OF LIGHT SHINES
FROM THE BIBLE

"I HAVE READ MANY BOOKS, BUT THE BIBLE READS ME."
—Author unknown

Estimates are that there are six Bibles in the average American home, yet few people in the twenty-first century really study the Word of God. To a generation saturated with the technological thrills of cable television, cell phone apps, Wi-Fi, the Internet, and computer games, the Holy Scriptures often appear uninteresting and boring. All too many who call themselves Christians simply believe what their church believes, rather than diligently studying the Scriptures for themselves to see what they believe. This reminds me of two men discussing the topic of religion.

"What do you believe about religion?" the first man asked.
"Oh, I believe what my church believes," his friend replied.
"Well then, what does your church believe?" the first man queried.
"Oh, my church believes what I believe," the second man responded.
Frustrated, the first man asked, "Then what do you and your church believe?"
His friend's final answer was, "Oh, that's easy. We both believe the same thing!"

Jesus Christ said, " 'Man shall not live by bread alone, but by every word that proceeds from the mouth of God' " (Matthew 4:4). In order to live by every word, we must desire to study every word. In these last days, Jesus wants us to be diligent students of the Scriptures. But for many who claim to be religious, this idea of "living by every word of God" is about as alien as a monster on Star Trek.

This must change if we are going to be prepared for the second coming of Jesus Christ.

Alonzo T. Jones and Ellet J. Waggoner were Seventh-day Adventist ministers who loved Jesus and carefully studied God's Book. They were also co-editors of a magazine called *Signs of the Times*. They took very seriously the counsel of the apostle Paul, "Be diligent to present yourself approved to God, a worker who does not need to be ashamed, rightly dividing the word of truth" (2 Timothy 2:15). They also accepted Paul's solemn charge to pastors, "Preach the word!" (2 Timothy 4:2). In their articles and preaching they tried to direct people away from human opinions, including their own, to the biblical "truth [as it] is in Jesus" (Ephesians 4:21). As mentioned earlier, these two men were key players at the landmark Seventh-day Adventist General Conference Session held in Minneapolis, Minnesota in 1888.

A certain R. T. Nash, who was also a delegate at the Minneapolis meeting, later reflected on the preaching of Jones and Waggoner at that conference. In his tract, *An Eye Witness Account*, Nash relayed a most interesting event.

> The writer of this little tract attended the Minneapolis conference in 1888 and saw and heard many of the various things that were done and said. Mrs. E. G. White from California was present, also Dr. E. J. Waggoner and Elder Alonzo T. Jones from California were there. It fell to the lot of Jones and Waggoner to conduct each morning the consecration services of the conference. . . . When Elders Jones and Waggoner came to reply to their opponents, they stood side by side with open Bibles.[1]

Nash then lists nineteen lengthy Scriptures, mostly from Romans and Galatians, that the two men read, one after another.

> "This was their answer without a word of comment; they took their seats. For the entire time of the reading there was hushed stillness over the vast assembly. This made an everlasting impression upon the writer that time can never efface."[2]

Ellen White was also one of the key players at the Minneapolis General Conference. She also loved Jesus and carefully studied God's Book. She was in that "vast assembly" listening to the preaching of Jones and Waggoner in 1888. In her letter entitled, "Looking Back At Minneapolis," she declared that what was preached by these two Californians was "the most precious light" shining from the Bible. Her words were, "At this meeting I bore testimony that the most precious light had been shining forth from the Scriptures in the presentation of the great subject of the righteousness of Christ connected with the law."[3] That "most precious light" that shone from the Bibles of Jones and Waggoner in 1888 can be found in our Bibles right now. If we are willing to search God's Book diligently, the same light will burst upon us today, in "the time of the end," when holy prophecy promises that "knowledge shall increase" (Daniel 12:4) in the hearts of God's children. If this is indeed our experience, then when by Heaven's light the earth is finally "illuminated with his glory" (Revelation 18:1), we will be lightened with it rather than being enveloped in darkness.

---

1. *Manuscripts and Memories of Minneapolis 1888* (Nampa, ID: Pacific Press®, 1988), 352.

2. Ibid., 354.

3. *Ellen G. White 1888 Materials* (Silver Spring, MD: Ellen G. White Estate, 1988), 212.

CHAPTER TWO

FOCUSING THE LENS

"TRUTH WILL ULTIMATELY PREVAIL
WHERE THERE ARE PAINS TO BRING IT TO LIGHT."
—George Washington (1731–1799),
first President of the United States of America

J ust as there are many versions of the Bible, so have there been various versions and interpretations of Jones and Waggoner's message by Adventist his-
torians, scholars and pastors. It is not my purpose to create a "New Revised
Standard 1888 Version." Every apple has a core, and it's time to discover the
core of their message so we can then study it from the Scriptures.

Adventist scholar Clinton Wahlen, in his meticulously researched article,
"What Did E. J. Waggoner Say at Minneapolis?" taken from chapter 1 of his
Master of Divinity thesis correctly declared, "E. J. Waggoner's lectures at the
Minneapolis General Conference are among the most important in all of Adventist history."[1] Wahlen reported that "Waggoner spoke at least twelve times
at Minneapolis. . . . On Monday, October 15, he began a series of at least nine
lectures on the law and its relationship to the righteousness of Christ."[2]

In the year 1888 there were no audio recorders or sophisticated video cam-
eras. Too bad. Waggoner's lectures were not captured, and we do not know his
exact words. Two other attendees, R. Dewitt Hottel and W. C. White, took
notes, "providing a good indication of his major points."[3]

But Ellen White was there, listening carefully to each of Waggoner's presentations. Near the end of the conference she gave an address titled, "A Call to a
Deeper Study of the Word," in which she made these significant statements:

> I see the beauty of the truth in the presentation of THE RIGHTEOUS-NESS OF CHRIST IN RELATION TO THE LAW as the Doctor [E. J. Waggoner] has placed it before us. . . . If our ministering brethren would accept the doctrine which has been presented so clearly—THE RIGH-TEOUSNESS OF CHRIST IN CONNECTION WITH THE LAW—and I know that they need to accept this, their prejudices would not have a controlling power, and the people would be fed with their portion of meat in due season.[4]

Here is the core of the message, stated twice. A few days later she said exactly the same thing two more times in her letter titled, "Looking Back At Minneapolis."

> Elder E. J. Waggoner had the privilege granted him of speaking plainly and presenting his views upon justification by faith and THE RIGHTEOUSNESS OF CHRIST IN RELATION TO THE LAW. This was no new light, but it was old light placed where it should be in the third angel's message. . . . At this meeting I bore testimony that the most precious light had been shining forth from the Scriptures in the presentation of THE GREAT SUBJECT OF THE RIGHTEOUS-NESS OF CHRIST CONNECTED WITH THE LAW, which should constantly be kept before the sinner as his only hope of salvation.[5]

Thus, four times within a few days Ellen White identified the essence of Waggoner's Minneapolis message as the righteousness of Christ in relation to the law, placed where it should be, in the third angel's message.

As we shall soon see, this is the golden key to unlock the mystery of Revelation 14:12. "Here is the patience of the saints; here are those who keep the commandments of God and the faith of Jesus."

The key is the perfect righteousness of Jesus Christ offered to every sinner as a free gift.

It's a gift we desperately need today.

---

1. Clinton Whalen, "Selected Aspects of Ellet J. Waggoner's Eschatology and Their Relation to His Understanding of Righteousness by Faith, 1882-1895" (Andrews University, July 1988), reported in the journal *Adventist Heritage*, vol. 13, no. 1 "Selected Aspects of Ellet J. Waggoner's Eschatology and Their Relation to His Understanding of Righteousness by Faith, 1882–1895," master's thesis, Andrews University, July 1988, p. 22.

2. Ibid., p. 28

3. Ibid.
4. *1888 Materials*, 164.
5. Ibid., 211, 212.

CHAPTER THREE

"This Message Will Lighten the Earth"

"ANGELS ARE SPIRITS, FLAMES OF FIRE; THEY ARE HIGHER THAN MAN,
THEY HAVE WIDER CONNECTIONS."
—Matthew Simpson (1811–1884),
American bishop of the Methodist Episcopal Church

Most humans are quite interested in supernatural beings, especially angels, and the Bible talks a lot about them. When Jesus was born in Bethlehem, an "angel of the Lord" appeared to a group of shepherds (Luke 2:9). After Christ was tempted in the wilderness by Satan, "angels came and ministered to Him" (Matthew 4:11). In the garden of Gethsemane, "an angel appeared to Him from heaven, strengthening Him" (Luke 22:43). On the morning of His resurrection, "there was a great earthquake; for an angel of the Lord descended from heaven, and came and rolled back the stone from the door, and sat on it. His countenance was like lightning, and his clothing as white as snow" (Matthew 28:2, 3).

The Bible plainly says that holy angels can still appear to people. Paul counseled Christians, "Do not forget to entertain strangers, for by so doing some have unwittingly entertained angels" (Hebrews 13:2).

In the year 1886, an angel appeared to Ellen White while she was traveling in Switzerland. His words are deeply significant, for they concern the third angel's message, which is the last message to be preached to fallen humanity before the return of Jesus Christ (compare Revelation 14:9–12 with verses 14–16).

Two years later in Minneapolis, in an address entitled, "To My Brethren Assembled At General Conference," Mrs. White divulged what the angel said.

> Two years ago, while in Switzerland, I was addressed in the night season by a voice which said, "Follow me.". . . . Many things were spoken which I will not now present to you. I was told that there was need of great spiritual revival among the men who bear responsibilities in the cause of God. . . . We must search the Scriptures for evidences of truth. "There are but few [said the angel], even of those who claim to believe it, that comprehend the third angel's message, and yet this is the message for this time. It is present truth. But how few take up this message in its true bearing, and present it to the people in its power! With many it has but little force."
>
> Said my guide, "THERE IS MUCH LIGHT YET TO SHINE FORTH FROM THE LAW OF GOD AND THE GOSPEL OF RIGHTEOUSNESS. THIS MESSAGE, UNDERSTOOD IN ITS TRUE CHARACTER AND PROCLAIMED IN THE SPIRIT, WILL LIGHTEN THE EARTH WITH ITS GLORY. The great decisive question is to be brought before all nations, tongues, and peoples. The closing work of the third angel's message will be attended with a power that will send the rays of the Sun of Righteousness into all the highways and byways of life, and decisions will be made for God as the supreme Governor; His law will be looked upon as the rule of His government."[1]

Thus the angel pinpointed the core of the third angel's message to be a spirit-filled proclamation of the law of God and the gospel of righteousness *combined.* According to the heavenly messenger, there is "much light" in "this message" of "the law of God and the gospel of righteousness." When this message "is understood in its true character and proclaimed in the Spirit,"[2] "the earth was illuminated with his glory" (Revelation 18:1).

If this is true—which it is—then is this not worthy of our careful study today?

No doubt.

---

1. *1888 Materials,* 165, 166.
2. Ibid.

CHAPTER FOUR

LUCIFER HATES "THIS TRUTH"

"THE HEART OF MAN IS THE PLACE THE DEVIL DWELLS IN."
—Sir Thomas Browne (1605–1682), English author

In addition to good angels, the Bible speaks about other angels that are no longer holy. The apostle Peter wrote about "the angels who sinned" (2 Peter 2:4). The leader of these fallen spirits is Lucifer (Isaiah 14:12), now called "the Devil and Satan, who deceives the whole world" (Revelation 12:9). Lucifer knows all about the third angel's message, for he is an angel himself. He also knows that more than a hundred years ago, one of his former friends appeared to Ellen White in Switzerland. He understands the message that will illuminate the earth with its glory (Revelation 18:1), *and he hates it.* As the book of Revelation states, one of his goals is to deceive the whole world (Revelation 12:9) about this very message.

When A. T. Jones and E. J. Waggoner preached the third angel's message in Minneapolis in 1888—centered in the righteousness of Jesus Christ—Lucifer himself was lurking in the shadows. Through his subtle maneuverings, he was able to influence certain leaders at that conference to oppose the very message the world so desperately needs. The following key paragraphs from the writings of Ellen White once again help us to focus the lens on what the core of that message really is and the deep opposition of the Prince of Darkness to God's truth.

In 1896, she wrote:

"The law was our schoolmaster to bring us unto Christ, that we might be justified by faith" (Galatians 3:24). In this scripture, the Holy Spirit through the apostle is speaking especially of the moral law. The law reveals sin to us, and causes us to feel our need of Christ and to flee unto Him for pardon and peace by exercising repentance toward God and faith toward our Lord Jesus Christ.

An unwillingness to accept this truth, lay at the foundation of a large share of the opposition manifested at Minneapolis against the Lord's message through brethren [E. J.] Waggoner and [A. T.] Jones. By exciting that opposition Satan succeeded in shutting away from our people, in a great measure, the special power of the Holy Spirit that God longed to impart to them. The enemy prevented them from obtaining that efficiency which might have been theirs in carrying the truth to the world, as the apostles proclaimed it after the day of Pentecost. The light that is to lighten the whole earth with its glory was resisted, and by the action of our own brethren has been in a great degree kept away from the world.[1]

These astonishing paragraphs reveal five amazing facts:

1. The core of the Minneapolis message, identified as "this truth," is once again seen as the proclamation of the law of God and the gospel of Jesus Christ *combined.*

2. There is in this message "the special power of the Holy Spirit" that will enable God's servants to "carry the truth to the world as the apostles proclaimed it after the day of Pentecost."

3. Satan "succeeded" in "shutting away from our people, in a great measure" this special power, which has in turn "been in a great degree kept away from the world."

4. The enemy succeeded through "the action of our own brethren." Note: Ellen White also clarified in 1896 that this "light" was "despised by some," not all.[2]

5. The message that was "resisted" was in fact the light that is to lighten the whole earth with its glory (see Revelation 18:1).

It was God's plan that the landmark Seventh-day Adventist General Conference Session in 1888 should become the epicenter of a spiritual earthquake that would eventually bring Satan's kingdom crashing down. The event could also be likened to the Allies' invasion of Normandy, which led to the downfall of Hitler's Third Reich. In 1888, God longed for Minneapolis to be His beachhead from which He would launch His final assault in Pentecostal power against the devil, leading to "the end of the world" (see Matthew 28:20). Realizing the ghastly potential for the destruction of his Evil Empire, Lucifer worked undercover strategically with infernal energy through human agents. Marshaling every resource of satanic skill and subtlety, the enemy "succeeded

. . . in a great measure" in hindering the message and in prolonging his own life.

Our enemy is still intensely committed to preventing God's heavenly message from being believed, received, experienced, and proclaimed to a lost world. We often see only on the surface of things. The crew on the Titanic saw only the tip of the iceberg above the surface of the water, yet it was the submerged portion that sank that mighty ship. So it is that Satan continues to work at this very moment underneath the waves of human influence to hinder and destroy God's message. Ellen White insightfully wrote,

> Much that has occurred since the Minneapolis meeting gives evidence of the working of things that lie deeper than human reason can fathom. . . . Much that has appeared on the surface as merely the design of men has had *its origin* in the schemes of the great Master worker of evil.[3]

Yes, Lucifer still hates *"this truth."*
By God's grace, it's time we shattered his deceptive wiles.

---

1. Ellen G. White, *Selected Messages* (Washington, DC: Review and Herald® Publishing Association, 1958), 1:234, 235.
2. See *Testimonies to Ministers,* 89.
3. *1888 Materials,* 1507.

CHAPTER FIVE

EXPLOSION AT MINNEAPOLIS

"EXTREMES ARE DANGEROUS."
—Jonathan Mayhew (1720–1766), noted American minister at Old West
Church, Boston, Massachusetts

As we have already seen, the third angel's message concludes with this: "Here is the patience of the saints: here are they that keep the commandments of God, and the faith of Jesus" (Revelation 14:12).

The pendulum between the law of God and the gospel of Christ has been swinging back and forth throughout Christian history. Many Jews in the time of Jesus claimed to follow Moses and the Ten Commandments, yet they rejected Christ as their Messiah and Savior. (See John 7:47–49.) The Protestant world today often goes to the opposite extreme. Many claim to follow Jesus while they reject the Ten Commandments. Ellen White put it this way: "The great sin of the Jews was their rejection of Christ; and the great sin of the Christian world would be their rejection of the law of God, the foundation of His government in heaven and earth."[1] Subject to temptation like everyone else, the Seventh-day Adventist Church has seen the pendulum swing back and forth throughout its history. In her letter, "Looking Back At Minneapolis," Ellen White summed up the failure of many Adventist ministers who had been stressing "the commandments of God" while neglecting "the faith of Jesus."

> The third angel's message is the commandments of God *and* the faith of Jesus Christ. The commandments of God have been proclaimed, but the faith of Jesus Christ has not been proclaimed by Seventh-day Adventists as *of equal importance,* the law and the gospel go hand in hand. I cannot find language to express this subject in its fullness.[2]

In the same letter she wrote,

> The faith of Jesus [preached by Jones and Waggoner] has been over-looked and treated in an indifferent, careless manner. It has not occu-pied the prominent position in which it was revealed to John. Faith in Christ as the sinner's only hope [the faith of Jesus] has been largely left out, not only of the discourses given but of the religious experience of very many who claim to believe the third angel's message.[3]

In a further critique of her fellow church members, Mrs. White moaned,

> Christ is left out of their sermonizing, and from east to west, from north to south, the church has been starving for the Bread of Life.[4]

Again,

> The law of God has been largely dwelt upon, and has been presented to congregations, almost as destitute of the knowledge of Jesus Christ and His relation to the law as was the offering of Cain.[5]

As we approach the "time of trouble, such as never was since there was a nation" (Daniel 12:1), the pendulum keeps swinging back and forth within the Church. Just as it was during the Minneapolis era, many today focus on the Ten Commandments but fail to stress "faith in Christ as the sinner's only hope." Others speak much about salvation by grace and the importance of having a "knowledge of Jesus Christ," yet they utterly fail to emphasize "His relation to the law" and our need of "keeping the commandments of God." We should beware of such imbalances. A preacher once said, "No lie is as successful as a half-truth." Another declared, "Be careful of half-truths; you might end up with the wrong half."

In the year 1888, in the city of Minneapolis, Minnesota, something won-derful happened. The pendulum centered. All heaven looked down with deep interest as a thirty-three-year-old preacher from California gave a series of lec-tures, mostly from Romans and Galatians.

Ellen White listened carefully, and then responded with her whole heart, "I see the beauty of the truth in the presentation of the righteousness of Christ in relation to the law as the Doctor [E. J. Waggoner] has placed it before us."[6] In a nutshell, the message of the Ten Commandments given amidst thunder and flame on Mount Sinai merged with the preaching of the cross of Jesus Christ and with His infinite sacrifice on Calvary. A spiritual explosion took place! Four years later, this word came from her inspired pen: "The time of test is just upon us, for the loud cry of the third angel has already begun in the revelation of the righteousness of Christ, the sin-pardoning Redeemer. This is the beginning of the light of the angel whose glory shall fill the whole earth."[7]

We need this explosion *right now.*

---

1. Ellen G. White, *The Great Controversy* (Mountain View, CA: Pacific Press®, 1911), 22.

2. *1888 Materials,* 217; emphasis supplied.

3. Ibid., 212.

4. Ibid., 891.

5. Ibid., 810.

6. Ibid., 164.

7. Ellen G. White, "The Perils and Privileges of the Last Days," *Review and Herald,* November 22, 1892.

CHAPTER SIX

"TAKE OFF YOUR SHOES—YOU ARE ON HOLY GROUND"

"NO MAN WILL RISE HIGH WHO JEERS AT SACRED THINGS."
—Author unknown

It is almost time to closely examine the details of God's last message, Christ our Righteousness, which is the third angel's message. We wish to do this carefully, and we want to do it primarily from the Bible. Select quotations will also be used from the writings of Ellen G. White, A. T. Jones and E. J. Waggoner during the era of the Minneapolis General Conference, simply because these three were key players that God used in a drama of cosmic significance. Compared with people like Bill Gates, Michael Jordan, or Oprah Winfrey, their incomes were peanuts. Nevertheless, as we ponder what they wrote and taught, we're in the big leagues.

Another reason we want to examine both the Bible and the writings of these long-dead people is that the book of Revelation says we should. Immediately following the description of the third angel's message comes this inspired counsel: "I heard a voice from heaven saying to me, 'Write: "Blessed are the dead who die in the Lord from now on." ' 'Yes,' says the Spirit, 'that they may rest from their labors, and *their works* follow them' " (Revelation 14:13; emphasis added). White, Jones, and Waggoner all taught the third angel's message. In the truths they wrote, "their works" still follow them.

The holy elements we are about to contemplate need to be mixed together like ingredients in a good meal. A skilled chef knows just how much oil, seasoning, or salt must be added in delicately balanced proportions to produce tasty results. Our heavenly Father is the Master Combiner. "As for God, His way is perfect" (2 Samuel 22:31). "His understanding is unsearchable" (Isaiah 40:28). Jesus alone knows exactly how to blend these elements into a perfect whole designed to finally produce His grandest goal—the preparation of "a people prepared for the Lord" (Luke 1:17).

For the record, I don't claim infallibility regarding the order or manner in which these elements are proclaimed. For some, only the love of Jesus Christ presented first can lead to a response of love for God and heart-felt obedience to His law. For others, only the Holy Spirit using the law first to shatter their self-confidence can lead to a heart appreciation for the love of Jesus Christ and the gospel. The theme of this book is that "the two blended" is Heaven's ordained channel for "the special power of the Holy Spirit." These Bible truths also reveal "the deep things of God" (1 Corinthians 2:10). Certainly God will continue teaching His chosen people advanced truths until the close of time, but such truths will always be in harmony with His previous teachings, and must be centered in Jesus.

"One thing I know" (John 9:25), each of us needs to humbly receive the truths we are about to zero in on, experience their power, and then by His grace, share them with others. I encourage you to spend time in prayerful, earnest, heart-searching meditation on these truths until your life is changed. When Moses drew near to a strange bush on Mount Sinai that burned but wasn't consumed, a voice spoke from the flames, "Take your sandals off your feet, for the place where you stand is holy ground" (Exodus 3:5).

Echoing the voice from Sinai, and in reference to this exact message, Ellen White testified, "Be careful how you treat it. Take off the shoes from off your feet; for you are on holy ground."[1]

This is wise advice.

---

1. White, *Testimonies to Ministers,* 89, 90.

CHAPTER SEVEN

Not Ten Suggestions, but Ten Commandments

"The Ten Commandments aren't prefaced with
'If you're in the mood.' "
—Dr. Laura Schlesinger (1947–),
American talk radio host, author, and socially conservative commentator

The Word of God declares, "For He will finish the work and cut it short in *righteousness,* because the Lord will make a short work upon the earth" (Romans 9:28; emphasis supplied). "He leads me in the paths of righteousness," wrote David, "for His name's sake" (Psalm 23:3). John wrote, "Little children, let no one deceive you. He who practices righteousness is righteous" (1 John 3:7). The angel in Switzerland declared that the final message concerns "the gospel of righteousness."[1] Ellen White identified it as the message of "the righteousness of Christ in relation to the law."[2]

What exactly is *righteousness*?

In 1890, E. J. Waggoner published a little tract titled, "Living By Faith," in which he made some insightful comments about Paul's use of the phrase "the righteousness of God" in Romans 1:17.

> This expression has been the subject of much learned discussion by theologians, and very few of them are agreed as to its meaning. The fact that learned men are disagreed in regard to it need not frighten us with the thought that it cannot be understood, for we read that things hidden from the wise and prudent are revealed unto babes. If we are but

simple enough to accept the obvious Scripture meaning, as explained by the Scriptures, we need not be in darkness.

One of the greatest causes of the failure of many people to understand the book of Romans, and, indeed, any other portion of Scripture, is a failure to hold to first principles and Bible definitions. Men attempt to define some terms according to their theological training, and find it hard work to make them fit. Then if they at any time accept the Bible definition of a term, they do not adhere to it, but give it some other meaning the next time they meet with it. This can lead to nothing else but confusion. The cause of the difficulty in understanding this text is a failure to cling to the Bible definition of the term "the righteousness of God." We have already seen that it is an expression indicating God's character, and that His character is set forth in the ten commandments.[3]

In his tract, Waggoner quoted many Scriptures, including the following, to prove from the Bible that God's righteousness is synonymous with the Ten Commandments: "All Your commandments are righteousness" (Psalm 119:172); and "Listen to Me, you who know righteousness, you people in whose heart is My law" (Isaiah 51:7). In the New Testament, Paul also wrote about "the law of righteousness" (Romans 9:31).

Ellen White agreed. "Righteousness is defined by the ten precepts given by the Lord on Mr. Sinai."[4] This is not an isolated statement. She often wrote about "God's great standard of righteousness, His holy law."[5] Waggoner echoed this idea. "The law of ten commandments, then, is the measure of the righteousness of God."[6] Elder Jones agreed 100 percent. "The commandments of God are the reflection, the transcript, the expression, of God's righteousness."[7]

It's no secret that people today are largely committed to doing their own thing. The popular philosophy, "If it feels good, do it," pops up in countless books, lyrics, posters, TV shows, and T-shirts. One best-selling book titled, *The Day America Told The Truth,* reveals the results of a massive survey taken coast to coast. The first chapter called, "A New Moral Authority In America: You're It!" reports that "there is absolutely no moral consensus at all [in this generation]. Everyone is making up their own moral codes—their own Ten Commandments."[8] The book then clarifies that "most Americans are very confused about their personal morals right now."[9] Sound familiar? It's the truth.

But God is not confused. He knows exactly what is right and what is wrong, and He has told us in His Word that we may know also. Essentially, the Ten Commandments show misguided human beings what is right, which is why this law is specifically identified as the law of righteousness. God's Law is righteous because He Himself is righteous, and His commandments are simply an expression of His moral nature. This is a golden truth we need to know. It is also part of the third angel's message that teaches "the commandments of God" (Revelation 14:12). This truth is part of our ABCs as we begin to study *God's Last Message: Christ Our Righteousness.*

Two years after the Minneapolis conference, Ellen White visited Washington, D.C. In the capital of our great nation, her thoughts turned toward the President of the Universe and the supreme importance of the Law of His government. In her diary she wrote,

> There is a necessity of dwelling upon the love of Jesus Christ; this is essential. But it is not all that must be spoken. The great standard of character—God's holy law, with all its solemn injunctions—should be distinctly set forth, together with the circumstances of the giving of the law from Mount Sinai in awful grandeur. The Lord Jesus Christ was there in person [compare Exodus 20:6 with John 14:15]. He spoke the law, and gave the commandments, which are unalterable, unchangeable, and eternal in their character.[10]

Based on this pointed counsel that "God's holy law . . . should be distinctly set forth, together with the circumstances of the giving of the law from Mount Sinai in awful grandeur," each of the Ten Commandments will be listed below, one by one, along with insightful comments from Ellen White taken from her book, *Patriarchs and Prophets,* from a chapter called, "The Law Given to Israel." As you read these solemn commandments, keep in mind that the Great I AM has never revealed Himself throughout fallen human history—ever!—with such visible manifestations of power and glory as on the day He spoke with His own voice His holy Ten Commandment law to more than a million former slaves He had just delivered from the land of Egypt. And His law is for us too.

Say a prayer before you read this.

THE CIRCUMSTANCES

"Then it came to pass on the third day, in the morning, that there were thunderings and lightnings, and a thick cloud on the mountain; and the sound of the trumpet was very loud, so that all the people who were in the camp trembled. And Moses brought the people out of the camp to meet with God, and they stood at the foot of the mountain. Now Mount Sinai was completely in smoke, because the Lord descended upon it in fire. Its smoke ascended like the smoke of a furnace, and the whole mountain quaked greatly" (Exodus 19:16–18).

THE FIRST COMMANDMENT

"And God spoke all these words, saying: 'I am the Lord your God, who brought

you out of the land of Egypt, out of the house of bondage. You shall have no other gods before Me' " (Exodus 20:1–3).

Jehovah, the eternal, self-existent, uncreated One, Himself the Source and Sustainer of all, is alone entitled to supreme reverence and worship. Man is forbidden to give to any other object the first place in his affections or his service. Whatever we cherish that tends to lessen our love for God or to interfere with the service due Him, of that do we make a god.[11]

THE SECOND COMMANDMENT

"You shall not make for yourself a carved image—any likeness of anything that is in heaven above, or that is in the earth beneath, or that is in the water under the earth; you shall not bow down to them nor serve them. For I, the Lord your God, am a jealous God, visiting the iniquity of the fathers upon the children to the third and fourth generations of those who hate Me" (Exodus 20:4, 5).

The second commandment forbids the worship of the true God by images or similitudes. Many heathen nations claimed that their images were mere figures or symbols by which the Deity was worshiped, but God has declared such worship to be sin. The attempt to represent the Eternal One by material objects would lower man's conception of God. The mind, turned away from the infinite perfection of Jehovah, would be attracted to the creature rather than to the Creator. And as his conceptions of God were lowered, so would man become degraded.[12]

"I, the Lord your God, am a jealous God" (Exodus 20:5).

"The close and sacred relation of God to His people is represented under the figure of marriage. Idolatry being spiritual adultery, the displeasure of God against it is fitly called jealousy."[13]

"Visiting the iniquity of the fathers upon the children to the third and fourth generations of those who hate Me" (Exodus 20:5).

It is inevitable that children should suffer from the consequences of parental wrongdoing, but they are not punished for the parents' guilt, except as they participate in their sins. It is usually the case, however, that children walk in the steps of their parents. By inheritance and example the sons become partakers of the father's sin. Wrong tendencies, perverted appetites, and debased morals, as well as physical disease and degeneracy, are transmitted as a legacy from father to son, to the third and fourth generation. This fearful truth should have a solemn power to restrain men from following a course of sin.[14]

"Showing mercy to thousands, to those who love Me and keep My command-ments" (Exodus 20:6).

In prohibiting the worship of false gods, the second commandment by implication enjoins the worship of the true God. And to those who are faithful in His service, mercy is promised, not merely to the third and fourth generation as is the wrath threatened against those who hate Him, but to thousands of generations.[15]

THE THIRD COMMANDMENT
"You shall not take the name of the Lord your God in vain, for the Lord will not hold him guiltless who takes His name in vain" (Exodus 20:7).

This commandment not only prohibits false oaths and common swearing, but it forbids us to use the name of God in a light or careless manner, without regard to its awful significance. By the thoughtless mention of God in common conversation, by appeals to Him in trivial matters, and by the frequent and thoughtless repetition of His name, we dishonor Him. "Holy and reverend is His name." Psalm 111:9. All should meditate upon His majesty, His purity and holiness, that the heart may be impressed with a sense of His exalted character; and His holy name should be uttered with reverence and solemnity.[16]

THE FOURTH COMMANDMENT
"Remember the Sabbath day, to keep it holy. Six days you shall labor and do all your work, but the seventh day is the Sabbath of the Lord your God. In it you shall do no work: you, nor your son, nor your daughter, nor your male servant, nor your female servant, nor your cattle, nor your stranger who is within your gates. For in six days the Lord made the heavens and the earth, the sea, and all that is in them, and rested the seventh day. Therefore the Lord blessed the Sabbath day and hallowed it" (Exodus 20:8–11).

The Sabbath is not introduced as a new institution but as having been founded at creation. It is to be remembered and observed as the memorial of the Creator's work. Pointing to God as the Maker of the heavens and the earth, it distinguishes the true God from all false gods.

All who keep the seventh day signify by this act that they are wor-shipers of Jehovah. Thus the Sabbath is the sign of man's allegiance to God as long as there are any upon the earth to serve Him. The fourth commandment is the only one of all the ten in which are found both the name and the title of the Lawgiver. It is the only one that shows by whose authority the law is given. Thus it contains the seal of God, affixed to His law as evidence of its authenticity and binding force. God has given men six days wherein to labor, and He requires that their own work be done in the six working days. Acts of necessity and mercy are permitted on the Sabbath, the sick and suffering are at all times to be cared for; but unnecessary labor is to be strictly avoided. "Turn away thy foot from the Sabbath, from doing thy pleasure on My holy day; and call the Sabbath a delight, the holy of the Lord, honorable; and . . . honor Him, not doing thine own ways, nor finding thine own plea-sure." Isaiah 58:13. Nor does the prohibition end here. "Nor speaking thine own words," says the prophet. Those who discuss business matters or lay plans on the Sabbath are regarded by God as though engaged in the actual transaction of business. To keep the Sabbath holy, we should not even allow our minds to dwell upon things of a worldly character. And the commandment includes all within our gates. The inmates of the house are to lay aside their worldly business during the sacred hours. All should unite to honor God by willing service upon His holy day.[17]

THE FIFTH COMMANDMENT
"Honor your father and your mother, that your days may be long upon the land which the Lord your God is giving you" (Exodus 20:12).

Parents are entitled to a degree of love and respect which is due to no other person. God Himself, who has placed upon them a responsibility for the souls committed to their charge, has ordained that during the earlier years of life, parents shall stand in the place of God to their chil-dren. And he who rejects the rightful authority of his parents is rejecting the authority of God. The fifth commandment requires children not only to yield respect, submission, and obedience to their parents, but also to give them love and tenderness, to lighten their cares, to guard their reputation, and to succor and comfort them in old age. It also enjoins respect for ministers and rulers and for all others to whom God has delegated authority.

This, says the apostle, "is the first commandment with promise." Ephesians 6:2. To Israel, expecting soon to enter Canaan, it was a pledge to the obedient, of long life in that good land; but it has a wider meaning, including all the Israel of God, and promising eternal life upon the earth when it shall be freed from the curse of sin.[18]

THE SIXTH COMMANDMENT
"You shall not murder" (Exodus 20:13).

All acts of injustice that tend to shorten life; the spirit of hatred and revenge, or the indulgence of any passion that leads to injurious acts toward others, or causes us even to wish them harm (for "whosoever hateth his brother is a murderer"); a selfish neglect of caring for the needy or suffering; all self-indulgence or unnecessary deprivation or excessive labor that tends to injure health—all these are, to a greater or less degree, violations of the sixth commandment.[19]

THE SEVENTH COMMANDMENT
"You shall not commit adultery" (Exodus 20:14).

This commandment forbids not only acts of impurity, but sensual thoughts and desires, or any practice that tends to excite them. Purity is demanded not only in the outward life but in the secret intents and emotions of the heart. Christ, who taught the far-reaching obligation of the law of God, declared the evil thought or look to be as truly sin as is the unlawful deed.[20]

THE EIGHTH COMMANDMENT
"You shall not steal" (Exodus 20:15).

Both public and private sins are included in this prohibition. The eighth commandment condemns manstealing and slave dealing, and forbids wars of conquest. It condemns theft and robbery. It demands strict integrity in the minutest details of the affairs of life. It forbids overreaching in trade, and requires the payment of just debts or wages. It declares that every attempt to advantage oneself by the ignorance, weakness, or misfortune of another is registered as fraud in the books of heaven.[21]

THE NINTH COMMANDMENT
"You shall not bear false witness against your neighbor" (Exodus 20:16).

False speaking in any matter, every attempt or purpose to deceive our neighbor, is here included. An intention to deceive is what constitutes falsehood. By a glance of the eye, a motion of the hand, an expression of the countenance, a falsehood may be told as effectually as by words. All intentional overstatement, every hint or insinuation calculated to convey an erroneous or exaggerated impression, even the statement of facts in such a manner as to mislead, is falsehood. This precept forbids every effort to injure our neighbor's reputation by misrepresentation or evil surmising, by slander or tale bearing. Even the intentional suppression of truth, by which injury may result to others, is a violation of the ninth commandment.[22]

THE TENTH COMMANDMENT

"You shall not covet your neighbor's house; you shall not covet your neighbor's wife, nor his male servant, nor his female servant, nor his ox, nor his donkey, nor anything that is your neighbor's" (Exodus 20:17).

The tenth commandment strikes at the very root of all sins, prohibiting the selfish desire, from which springs the sinful act. He who in obedience to God's law refrains from indulging even a sinful desire for that which belongs to another will not be guilty of an act of wrong toward his fellow creatures.[23]

ISRAEL'S RESPONSE

"Now all the people witnessed the thunderings, the lightning flashes, the sound of the trumpet, and the mountain smoking; and when the people saw it, they trembled and stood afar off. Then they said to Moses, 'You speak with us, and we will hear; but let not God speak with us, lest we die.' And Moses said to the people, 'Do not fear; for God has come to test you, and that His fear may be before you, so that you may not sin' " (Exodus 20:18–20).

Such were the sacred precepts of the Decalogue, spoken amid thunder and flame, and with a wonderful display of the power and majesty of the great Lawgiver. God accompanied the proclamation of His law with exhibitions of His power and glory, that His people might never forget the scene, and that they might be impressed with profound veneration for the Author of the law, the Creator of heaven and earth. He would also show to all men the sacredness, the importance, and the permanence of His law.[24]

As we approach Earth's last crisis, spiritually bankrupt partygoers often plan gigantic New Year's Eve bashes around the globe. Each year, when 11:59 p.m. on December 31 clicks over to midnight, fireworks blast off in New York, Los Angeles, London, Moscow, Paris, and Rome. But what is this in comparison with that awesome moment when the voice of God once again booms "from [His] throne, saying, 'It is done!' And there were noises and thunderings and lightnings; and there was a great earthquake, such a mighty and great earthquake as had not occurred since men were on the earth" (Revelation 16:17–18)?

Tragically, when this time finally strikes, the party will be over for the majority of earth's teeming masses who have taken no interest in "the commandments of God and the faith of Jesus" (Revelation 14:12).

In 1893, A. T. Jones reflected on a conversation a certain Brother Starr had with Ellen White about the giving of the law on Mount Sinai.

> She saw that the angels, ten thousand times ten thousand, and thousands of thousands, surrounded the people of God as they assembled around the mountain, and all above them, thus making a great living tabernacle from which every evil angel was excluded; and that not one word that was to come from the voice of Jesus should be altered in any mind, or one suggestion of doubt or evil, to a soul, be made.[25]

The Bible reports that shortly after God verbally proclaimed the Ten Commandments to Israel and to the world, He took a monumental step to preserve His righteousness for all generations. "When He had made an end of speaking with him on Mount Sinai, He gave Moses two tablets of the Testimony, tablets of stone, *written with the finger of God*" (Exodus 31:18; emphasis supplied).

The Bible is a sacred book, but it was still written by men. The Ten Commandments are an exception. They are unique, separate from any other set of words, being written not with a pen, stylus, or computer keyboard but "with the finger of God." Honestly, dear reader, if you wish to find fault with any part of the Lord's Book—which I don't recommend—let it not be with the only part God Himself wrote with His finger on solid rock! And remember, Moses did not come down from Mount Sinai with ten suggestions but with Ten Commandments *"which He commanded you to perform"* (Deuteronomy 4:13; emphasis supplied).

There is another biblical definition that is absolutely essential for us to understand in order to grasp God's final message. It is the definition of sin. If we make a mistake here, it can be as serious as taking a wrong turn in a series of dark tunnels in an underground cave. We will become lost and may never find our way back to the light. Immediately following the giving of the law upon Mount Sinai, "Moses said to the people, 'Do not fear; for God has come to test you, and that His fear may be before you, so that you may not sin' " (Exodus 20:20).

Moses' words inform us that the way to "not sin" is to obey the Ten Commandments. The New Testament agrees perfectly: "Sin is lawlessness" (1 John 3:4). Paul stated plainly, "I would not have known sin except through the law. For I would not have known covetousness unless the law had said, 'You shall not covet' " (Romans 7:7).

Ellen White agreed with Moses, John, and Paul. "What is to bring the sinner to the knowledge of his sins unless he knows what sin is? The only definition of sin in the Word of God is given us in 1 John 3:4: 'sin is the transgression of the law.' "[26] "There should be a clear understanding of that which constitutes sin, and we should avoid the least approach to step over the boundaries from obedience to disobedience."[27] If only Adam and Eve had learned this lesson before they chose to taste forbidden fruit! Which commandment did they break in the Garden of Eden? How about, "You shall have no other gods before Me" (Exodus 20:3)?

E. J. Waggoner wrote,

> There is no sin either of word, deed, or thought which the law of God will not search out and condemn. How necessary, then, that we make it our constant study! As we do not wish to cherish sin, and thus fail of eternal life, we must understand in all cases just what sin is; and to this end let us never cease to pray, with the Psalmist, "Open thou mine eyes, that I may behold wondrous things out of thy law."[28]

Through the special enlightenment of the Holy Spirit we can also discover the vital fact that "the law is spiritual" (Romans 7:14). Jesus Christ Himself taught this when He revealed that the Ten Commandments apply not only to outward actions but also to the thoughts and intents of the heart. If a man merely "looks at a woman to lust for her," Jesus clarified, he has "committed adultery with her already in his heart" (Matthew 5:28), even if he never slips into a bed with her. John also wrote, "Whoever hates his brother is a murderer" (1 John 3:15). It is a solemn truth that:

> God's law reaches to the internal as well as to the external actions of men. It is a discerner of the thoughts and intents and purposes of the soul. A man may be guilty of sins which God alone knows. God's law is indeed a searcher of hearts. There are dark passions of jealousy and revenge and hatred and malignity, lust, and wild ambition that are covered from human observation, and the great I AM knows it all. Sins have been contemplated and yet not carried out for want of opportunity. God's law makes a record of all these. These hidden-away, secret sins form character.[29]

"God is love" (1 John 4:16). While we may have a difficult time understanding this, in the highest sense, the Ten Commandment law is a law of love. God's law is designed to form a wall of protection around us to keep us from harm, and as a safeguard to our happiness. Make no mistake about it: it is sin that destroys human souls, not the law. Because God loves us so much, He Himself came down on Mount Sinai to write out His law of righteousness with His own finger. He wants us to know exactly what sin is, and to avoid it. Ellen White agreed perfectly:

"His nature, His law, is love."[30] "The law of God is an expression of His very nature; it is an embodiment of the great principle of love, and hence is the foundation of His government in heaven and earth."[31]

In the New Testament, Jesus Christ summarized what it means to genuinely keep the Ten Commandments when He said (quoting Moses),

" ' "You shall love the Lord your God with all your heart, with all your soul, and with all your mind." This is the first and great commandment. And the second is like it: "You shall love your neighbor as yourself" ' " (Matthew 22:37–39).

To keep the first four commandments we must truly love the Lord our God with all our heart. To keep the last six, we must love our neighbor as ourselves. Now think carefully. If loving God is "the first and great commandment," and if sin is "lawlessness" (1 John 3:4), then failing to love God with our whole being must be the greatest sin of all.

An apple may look good on the outside and yet be rotten at its core. A man or woman may look healthy on the outside, yet deep within the colon, prostate, liver, pancreas, lungs, or brain, deadly cancer cells may be multiplying rapidly. So it is with many who " 'outwardly appear righteous to men, but inside . . . are full of hypocrisy and lawlessness' " (Matthew 23:28). Just as God's last message, which is Christ our Righteousness, has a core, even so is there an inner core to our sin problem. What is it? The tenth commandment, "You shall not covet" (Exodus 20:17), reaches even to one's feelings. As we saw earlier, Ellen White commented, "The tenth commandment strikes at the very root of all sins, prohibiting the selfish desire, from which springs the sinful act."[32] With whom did this "very root of all sins" begin? "Sin originated in self seeking. Lucifer, the covering cherub, desired to be first in heaven."[33] Thus sin originated when a holy angel cherished an evil desire in his heart to be first, to be number one—in short, to replace God Himself. As sin developed, it eventually led to a very real and bitter war in heaven (Revelation 12:7) between Jesus Christ and this angel who became a devil. After Adam and Eve sinned, Satan's "selfish desire" entered humanity. It's not hard to see. Just look around. Isn't it natural for people to want to be number one? Author Robert Ringer even wrote a best-selling book called *Looking Out For #1*. When Adam sinned, "selfishness took the place of love."[34] Literally billions throughout history, infected with Lucifer's spirit, have been "lovers of their own selves" (2 Timothy 3:2).

It's a scary thought, but the truth is that selfishness often lies hidden in the subterranean depths of human hearts. A few days after the Minneapolis conference, Ellen White wrote, "Self has far more to do with our religious experience than we imagine."[35] In 1888 Satan worked mysteriously through the selfishness of some of the delegates and succeeded in hindering the message. "At Minneapolis . . . they would have had a rich experience. But self said, No."[36] She tried to warn the delegates of the subtle influence of their invisible foe. "The lower we lie at the foot of the cross the more clear will be our view of Christ. For just as soon as we begin to lift ourselves up and to think that we are something, the view of Christ grows dimmer and dimmer and Satan steps in so that we cannot see Him at all."[37] As it was then, so it is now. And behold, "The lover of self is a transgressor of the law."[38]

As the angel said to Ellen White in Switzerland, "There is much light yet to shine forth from the law of God."[39] It is my hope that some of this "light" now shines into your heart. As the Holy Spirit searches the hidden spiritual arteries of our souls, does He see the malignant cancer cells of selfishness lurking there? If so, we have "become *a transgressor* of the law" (James 2:11; emphasis supplied). The Bible tells the truth: "All have sinned" (Romans 3:23). Paralleling the AIDS epidemic, the Heavenly Physician has diagnosed us all as "SIN positive." We're all in this together. All are guilty of breaking the Ten Commandments, the Law of Righteousness, the Law of love—the foundation of God's government in heaven and on earth.

---

1. *1888 Materials*, 166.

2. Ibid., 164.

3. E. J. Waggoner, "Living By Faith," 9–10, reprinted by Laymen Ministries, 2010.

4. Ellen G. White, *Steps to Christ* (Battle Creek, MI: Review and Herald®, 1892), 61.

5. Ellen G. White, *Christ's Object Lessons* (Oakland, CA: Pacific Press®, 1900), 314.

6. E. J. Waggoner, *Christ and His Righteousness* (Oakland, CA: Pacific Press®, 1890), 48.

7. *1893 General Conference Bulletin*, 245.

8. James Patterson and Peter Kim, *The Day America Told the Truth* (New York: Prentice Hall, 1991), 25.

9. Ibid., 34.

10. *1888 Materials,* 781.

11. Ellen G. White, *Patriarchs and Prophets* (Oakland, CA: Pacific Press®, 1890), 305.

12. Ibid., 306.

13. Ibid.

14. Ibid.

15. Ibid.

16. Ibid.

17. Ibid., 307.

18. Ibid., 308.

19. Ibid.

20. Ibid.

21. Ibid., 309.

22. Ibid.

23. Ibid.

24. Ibid.

25. *1893 General Conference Bulletin,* 377.

26. *1888 Materials,* 780.

27. White, *Selected Messages,* 1:234.

28. E. J. Waggoner, *Signs of the Times,* October 12, 1891.

29. *1888 Materials,* 374.

30. White, *Patriarchs and Prophets,* 33.

31. White, *Steps to Christ,* 60.

32. White, *Patriarchs and Prophets,* 309.

33. White, *The Desire of Ages,* 21.

34. White, *Steps to Christ,* 17.

35. *1888 Materials,* 215.

36. Ibid., 1030.

37. *1888 Materials,* 159.

38. Ellen G. White, *Thoughts From the Mount of Blessing* (Oakland, CA: Pacific Press®, 1896), 79.

39. *1888 Materials,* 166.

CHAPTER EIGHT

THE LAW SAYS, "GO TO JESUS CHRIST!"

"MANY OF THE INSIGHTS OF SAINTS
STEM FROM THEIR EXPERIENCE AS SINNERS."
—Eric Hoffer (1902–1983),
American author, awarded the Presidential Medal of Freedom

The apostle Paul wrote, "The law was our tutor to bring us to Christ" (Galatians 3:24). Ellen White identified this exact text as "this truth . . . at Minneapolis . . . the Lord's message through Brethren [E. J.] Waggoner and [A. T.] Jones."[1] Paul also taught "this truth" in the seventh chapter of Romans when he testified how the Holy Spirit used the law of God to convict him—a self-righteous Pharisee—of his own sins, and to lead him to Christ. "I would not have known sin except through the law. . . . When the commandment came, sin revived and I died . . . that sin through the commandment might become exceedingly sinful. For we know that the law is spiritual, but I am carnal, sold under sin" (Romans 7:7, 9, 13, 14).

Commenting on Paul's experience described in Romans 7, Ellen White wrote,

> When the spiritual character of the law was discerned, he [Paul] saw himself a sinner. . . . When he looked into the depths of its holy precepts, and saw himself as God saw him, he bowed in humiliation and confessed his guilt. . . . When he saw the spiritual nature of the law, sin appeared in its true hideousness, and his self-esteem was gone.[2]

This holy revelation led Paul to cry out, "O wretched man that I am! Who will deliver me from this body of death?" (Romans 7:24). Then he found the answer and proclaimed, "I thank God—through Jesus Christ our Lord!" (Romans 7:25).

Contrary to popular opinion, Paul wrote much about the divinely ordained function of the law as a "tutor to bring us to Christ" (Galatians 3:24). In Galatians 3:23 he further explained, "Before faith came, we were kept under guard by the law, kept for the faith which would afterward be revealed." A year before the Minneapolis conference, E. J. Waggoner commented on this exact verse. Notice carefully:

> It is the law which arrests the criminal; the sheriff is simply the visible agent of the law. It is the law which locks the prisoner in his cell; the jailer, the iron walls, and heavy bars which surround the prisoner, are simply the emblems of the iron hand of the law which is upon him. . . . So it is with the sinner against God's government. The eyes of the Lord are in every place, so that there is no possibility that he can escape arrest. As soon as he has sinned, he is seized by the law, and is at once under condemnation of death. . . . Now he is shut in on every side by the law. There is not one of the commandments which is not against him, because there is not a man on earth who has not broken every one of them.
>
> The Spirit of God causes the prison walls to close in upon him, his cell becomes narrower and narrower, and he feels oppressed; and then he makes desperate struggles to escape. He starts out in one way, but there the first commandment rises up against him and will not let him go free. He turns in another direction, but he has taken the name of God in vain, and the third commandment refuses to let him get his liberty in that direction. . . . So with all the commandments. They utterly refuse to grant him liberty, because he has violated every one of them. . . . He is completely shut in on every side. There is, however, just one avenue of escape, and that is through Christ. Christ is the door (John 10:9), and entrance through that door gives freedom (John 8:36).[3]

In a *Signs* article, "Comments on Galatians 3, No. 8," Waggoner expressed the same thought about verse 23:

> He (the sinner) is absolutely "shut up" to the faith which may afterwards be revealed as the only means of escape from present guilt, and from the wrath to come. . . . Stung by his awakened conscience, the guilty one seeks peace and rest, but the law relentlessly charges him

with his sin. All that it will do is deepen conviction, and thus add to the load that weighs down the sinner. Finally, when he loses confidence in himself, and cries out, "O wretched man that I am," he is forced to cast himself at the feet of Jesus, saying, "Lord be merciful to me, a sinner." This is the only avenue of escape, and it is one that never fails. Thus the law literally drives the sinner to Christ, by shutting up every other way of freedom from guilt.[4]

Waggoner's pointed, insightful explanation of Galatians 3:23 and 24 perfectly parallel Ellen White's use of Galatians 3:24 to summarize "this truth" of Waggoner's message at Minneapolis, which was Paul's message, which is also a key component of the third angel's message. Read it again:

> "The law was our schoolmaster to bring us unto Christ, that we might be justified by faith." (Galatians 3:24). . . . The law reveals sin to us, and causes us to feel our need of Christ and to flee unto Him for pardon and peace by exercising repentance toward God and faith toward our Lord Jesus Christ.
>
> An unwillingness to . . . accept this truth, lay at the foundation of a large share of the opposition manifested at Minneapolis against the Lord's message through Brethren [E. J.] Waggoner and [A. T.] Jones.[5]

In another *Signs* article, "Comments on Galatians 3, No. 3," Waggoner's main text was, "What purpose then does the law serve?" (Galatians 3:19). His comments included an explanation of what Paul wrote in Romans 5:20: "The law entered that the offense might abound. But where sin abounded, grace abounded much more." Waggoner wrote,

> The "entering" of the law was at Sinai. Why did it enter? . . . It was then formally given that the enormity of sin might be seen. Says Paul, "But where sin abounded, grace did much more abound . . ." That is, it was necessary for men to see the real nature of sin, in order that they might seek the grace that is in Christ, which alone can take away sin. And the more enormous sin appeared, the more comprehensive views could they have of grace. For no matter how greatly sin abounded, grace super-abounded.[6]

To put it simply, *the Ten Commandments were given on Mt. Sinai to show us that we are sinners who need Jesus Christ.* The following paragraphs written by Ellen White beautifully summarize "this truth" that we all need today:

The first step in reconciliation to God is the conviction of sin. "Sin is the transgression of the law." "By the law is the knowledge of sin" (1 John 3:4; Romans 3:20). In order to see his guilt, the sinner must test his character by God's great standard of righteousness. It is a mirror which shows the perfection of a righteous character and enables him to discern the defects of his own. . . .

"The Law of the Lord is perfect, converting the soul" (Psalm 19:7). Without the law, men have no just conception of the purity and holiness of God or of their own guilt and uncleanness. They have no conviction of sin and feel no need of repentance. Not seeing their lost condition as violators of God's law, they do not feel their need of the atoning blood of Christ.[7]

At this moment most human beings are in this exact condition, feeling no need for a Savior. Their plight is like a man floating peacefully down a river on a raft. Yet unknown to the naive traveler, just around the next bend is a thousand-foot waterfall that he does not see and feels no need to avoid. As we approach "the great day of the LORD" that "hastens quickly" (Zephaniah 1:14), earth's teeming billions have no idea that soon, God, the Judge of all, will require an account from them for "every transgression" of His holy Law (Hebrews 2:2; Romans 14:12; Ecclesiastes 12:13, 14).

Who will wake them up?

If not now, *when*? If not you, *who*?

Someone is trying to arouse sinners today. He is the Holy Spirit. His love for lost humans is too great for Him to remain silent while so many are in peril. Jesus said, "When He [the Spirit of Truth] has come, He will convict the world of sin, and of righteousness, and of judgment" (John 16:8). Unlike many compromising preachers, the Spirit of God isn't afraid to step on toes. He loves us too much. And He is not seeking to win any popularity contests either. His influence is described in the following quotation.

But when the heart yields to the influence of the Spirit of God, the conscience will be quickened, and the sinner will discern something of the depth and sacredness of God's holy law, the foundation of His government in heaven and on earth. The "Light, which lighteth every man that cometh into the world," illumines the secret chambers of the soul, and the hidden things of darkness are made manifest. John 1:9. Conviction takes hold upon the mind and heart. The sinner has a sense of the righteousness of Jehovah and feels the terror of appearing, in his own guilt and uncleanness, before the Searcher of hearts.[8]

How is it with you, my friend? Is your heart open to the deep moving of the Spirit of the Lord? Is He using the law to lead you to Christ? Do you sense your desperate need for a Savior?

When I visited New Zealand in 1993, I often saw sheep grazing peacefully on mountains. From a distance, against the backdrop of the green grass, their wool looked perfectly white and clean. Yet when the pure white snow from heaven covers the ground, the same wool appears much dirtier, *as it really is.*

In the same way, when we compare ourselves with a moral law that is "holy and just and good" (Romans 7:12), we see ourselves as we really are—unclean in His sight. The popular phrase, "I'm OK, you're OK," is a lie. We're not OK. We are lost sinners *who need Jesus Christ.*

I will conclude this chapter with the words of John Wesley, seventeenth-century founder of the Methodist Church, quoted by E. J. Waggoner in *Signs.* While Wesley's words may not be popular today, they are in perfect harmony with the Word of God.

> It is the ordinary method of the Spirit of God to convict sinners by the law. It is this, which being set home on the conscience, generally breaketh the rock in pieces. It is more especially this part of the word of God which is "quick and powerful," full of life and energy, and "sharper than any two-edged sword." This, in the hand of God and of those whom He hath sent, pierces through all the folds of a deceitful heart, and "divides asunder soul and spirit;" yea, as it were, "joints and marrow." By this is the sinner discovered to himself. All his fig leaves are torn away, and he sees that he is "wretched, and poor, and miserable, and blind, and naked." The law flashes conviction on every side. He feels himself a mere sinner. His "mouth is stopped," and he stands "guilty before God."
>
> To slay the sinner is then the first use of the law; to destroy the life and strength wherein he trusts, and convince him that he is dead while he liveth, not only under the sentence of death, but actually dead unto God, void of all spiritual life, "dead in trespasses and sins." The second use of it is to bring him unto life—unto Christ that he may live. It is true, in performing both these offices, it acts the part of a severe schoolmaster. It drives by force, rather than draws us by love. And yet love is the spring of it all. It is the spirit of love which, by this painful means, tears away our confidence in the flesh, which leaves us no broken reed whereon to trust, and so constrains the sinner, stripped of all, to cry out in the bitterness of his soul, or groan in the depth of his heart—"I give up every plea beside, Lord, I am damned, but Thou has died."[9]

Though he's dead, Wesley's "works" (see Revelation 14:13) still speak.

---

1. White, *Selected Messages,* 1:234.

2. White, *Steps to Christ,* 29, 3.

3. E. J. Waggoner, *The Gospel in the Book of Galatians* (Oakland, CA: unknown publisher, 1888), 37.

4. E. J. Waggoner, "Comments on Galatians 3, No. 8," *Signs of the Times,* Aug. 26, 1886.

5. White, *Selected Messages,* 1:234.

6. E. J. Waggoner, "Comments on Galatians 3, No. 3," *Signs of the Times,* July 22, 1886.

7. White, *The Great Controversy,* 467, 468.

8. White, *Steps to Christ,* 24.

9. E. J. Waggoner, *Signs of the Times,* September 2, 1886.

CHAPTER NINE

"MR. LAW, WILL YOU PLEASE JUSTIFY ME?" "NO."

"HE WHO SPARES THE GUILTY THREATENS THE INNOCENT."
—legal maxim

Paul said plainly, "By the deeds of the law no flesh will be justified in His sight" (Romans 3:20) and "a man is not justified by the works of the law" (Galatians 2:16). This clear truth is also a part of the third angel's message. To illustrate, imagine a man who is arrested for murder. A year later he is brought to trial.

"Are you guilty?" inquires the judge.

"Yes, Your Honor, but that was a year ago. I have kept the law from that time until now. Will you not justify me?"

The answer will be an emphatic, "*No.*"

"But I have been *so* good," the prisoner pleads. "I have cleaned my cell, scrubbed the halls, and helped cook meals for other prisoners. Won't you please justify me?"

"No!" again.

Period. That's final.

In other words, no amount of obedience can remove the guilt of a past crime.

In like manner, when we violate the Ten Commandments, we are "guilty before God" (Romans 3:19). The third commandment states, "The Lord will not hold him guiltless who takes His name in vain" (Exodus 20:7). This guilt applies to breaking any one of the commandments. "For whoever shall keep the whole law, and yet stumble in one point, he is guilty of all" (James 2:10). It is impossible to get rid of this guilt by our own efforts at trying to be good. Absolutely no amount of present or future obedience can remove the guilt of even one sin. It's no use. God's law won't let us off the hook. "Therefore" explained Paul, "by the deeds of the law no flesh will be justified in His sight" (Romans 3:20).

In other words, once the Spirit of God has finally reached us and convicted us that we are lawbreakers, we simply cannot squirm out of our guilt even by deciding to turn around and obey the Ten Commandments. Even if we attempt to do it "by grace." A sign on a freeway once said, "If you're going the wrong direction, God allows U-turns." He does. But if we are seeking to remove our guiltiness by turning around and keeping the law, we are still "going the wrong direction." It can't be done. "No flesh" means no one. Not you, not me, not anyone. Once we are guilty of breaking the Big Ten, we cannot receive one iota of righteousness, salvation, or deliverance from the law. In fact, boasting about our supposed obedience will only increase our guilt. The beast has "a mouth speaking great things" (Revelation 13:5), and he isn't the only one. The whole world loves to talk and try to make self look good. Yet the third angel teaches us that "whatever the law says, it says to those who are under the law, that every mouth may be stopped, and all the world may become guilty before God" (Romans 3:19). Hitler told Germany, "Stop thinking, and follow me." God is telling the world, "Stop talking, and listen to Me." Before His law, our chattering lips are "stopped" (Romans 3:19). We are "kept under guard by the law" (Galatians 3:23). Period. End of discussion. We can all learn a lesson from a wise owl. "A wise old owl sat in an oak. The more he saw, the less he spoke. The less he spoke, the more he heard. Now wasn't he a wise old bird?"

Paul wrote, "By the law is the knowledge of sin" (Romans 3:20). Thus the law's function is to convict us, not forgive us. While the law is righteous, it cannot transfer any of its righteousness to us. Not one iota. The law was written by the finger of God upon a rock, and we can't get righteousness from a rock. Yet many try. Paul opposed such efforts in no uncertain terms, seeing in these very efforts a blatant challenge to the gospel. He countered, "If righteousness comes through the law, then Christ died in vain" (Galatians 2:21). Again, "If there had been a law given which could have given life, truly righteousness would have been by the law. But the Scripture has confined all under sin, that the promise by faith in Jesus Christ might be given to those who believe" (Galatians 3:21, 22).

At the 1893 General Conference Session, A. T. Jones confessed that this same misconception had become a serious problem for many Seventh-day Adventists.

The righteousness of God as expressed in letters, in words, in the ten commandments, is the law of God. Now, all agree with that; there is not a Seventh-day Adventist that will not agree with that. The difficulty is, so many people try to get the righteousness of God out of the law by the law. Some try to get it—no; they actually get it without the law, by the faith of Jesus Christ.[1]

Taking his stand with Jones, Waggoner wrote this excellent summary in the *Signs:*

> The case, then, stands thus: The law demands perfect and unvarying obedience, but it speaks to all the world and finds none righteous; all have violated it, and all are condemned by it. Romans 3:9-19. Present or future obedience will not take away past transgression, therefore the law cannot help us.[2]

In another pointed article titled, "No Justification by the Law," Waggoner commented on Romans 3:19, 20:

> A doer of the law is one who has always done it. If a man has failed in only one particular, he cannot be called a doer of the law, for the simple reason that he hasn't done it all. Therefore on this account he can never be justified by the law.[3]

Ellen White agreed with the apostle Paul, Waggoner, and Jones in a significant article titled, "Experience Following the 1888 Minneapolis Conference; The Danger Of Legalism; Emphasizing Religious Liberty." She wrote,

> By the deeds of the law shall no flesh be justified. There is no power in the law to save the transgressor of the law. If man, after his transgression, could have been saved by his utmost energy to keep the law, then Jesus need not have died.[4]

At this point it is of vital consequence that we correctly understand the biblical meaning of the word justification. Ellen White warned, "The danger has been presented to me again and again of entertaining, as a people, false ideas of justification by faith. I have been shown that Satan would work is a special manner to confuse the mind on this point."[5] The third angel's message is a special subject, which explains why the devil works masterfully in a "special manner" to confuse human minds "on this point." He knows that the special power of the Holy Spirit is involved here. He listened when the good angel informed Ellen White in Switzerland, "This message, understood in its true character, and proclaimed in the Spirit, will lighten the earth with its glory."[6]

Satan is his name. Confusion is his game.

Let's look carefully at Romans 3 again. Paul clarified in Romans 3:19 that in the light of the Law, the entire world is "guilty before God." Then in verse 20 he wrote, "By the law is the knowledge of sin." Verse 23 states, "All have sinned." Then verse 24 says we are "justified freely by His grace." Here we have a sequence. The Law reveals our sin and guilt, leading to justification by His grace. Justification, then, is justification from our sins of breaking the law. Then we are no longer "guilty before God" (Romans 3:19). This is exactly what Waggoner believed. He wrote in the *Signs,* "Justification has reference to the moral law. From the transgression of that, man needs justification; but the law cannot justify any sinner, it can only condemn. And so it drives him to Christ, that he may be justified by faith."[7]

Romans 4:5 speaks of how God "justifies the ungodly." Then Romans 4:7, 8 defines justification, which can only be received by grace. "Blessed are those whose lawless deeds are forgiven, and whose sins are covered; blessed is the man to whom the Lord shall not impute sin." These Scriptures reveal that to be justified simply means to be forgiven, with our sins covered. It means that God does "not impute sin" to us even though we have broken His Ten Commandments. That justification is the same thing as forgiveness is plainly taught in Acts 13:38, 39.

> Therefore let it be known to you, brethren, that through this Man [Jesus] is preached to you the forgiveness of sins; and by Him everyone who believes is justified from all things from which you could not be justified by the law of Moses.

Again Waggoner agreed. "What brings justification, or the forgiveness of sins? It is faith."[8] Jesus Christ taught the same truth when He told the parable of the proud Pharisee and the contrite tax collector in Luke 18:9–14. When the needy tax collector cried out, " 'God, be merciful to me a sinner,' " Jesus replied, " 'I tell you, this man went down to his house justified rather than the other' " (Luke 18:14). The tax collector was justified from his sins of breaking the law when he received mercy from God. But the proud Pharisee was not justified; therefore, his guilt remained. Jesus also solemnly stated, " 'By your words you will be justified, and by your words you will be condemned' " (Matthew 12:37).

Here again, justification is proven to be the opposite of condemnation.

Ellen White was crystal clear on the meaning of justification, and she agreed with Jesus, Paul, and E. J. Waggoner. After quoting Romans 3:24–26, she wrote, "Justification and pardon are one and the same thing. . . . Justification is the opposite of condemnation. . . . Justification is a full, complete pardon of sin."[9] Again, "As the penitent sinner, contrite before God, discerns Christ's atonement in his behalf, and accepts this atonement as his only hope in this life and the future life, his sins are pardoned. This is justification by faith."[10]

How much clearer can it be? It's simple. Justification is forgiveness, a full and complete pardon, the removal of guilt, and the opposite of condemnation. A. T. Jones once said, "It is so, because the Bible says so." Once again, this is a solid biblical truth that is part of our ABCs as we study this truth of the third angel's message.

God's Word is plain. No human being can ever be justified from his sins of breaking the Big Ten by his own puny efforts to obey the law. We simply cannot be forgiven, with our sins covered, by our works. No amount of obedience can remove a particle of guilt. Neither can we do anything to earn or merit the blessedness of a full, complete pardon of sin.Not a chance. God cannot be bribed.

Billions of dollars are spent by advertising gurus to discover what appeals to human hearts. Once I saw a billboard advertising a brand of cigarettes called "Merit." Beside a man holding a pack of cigarettes, the caption stated in bold letters, "You've Got Merit." We naturally want merit. It is part of our selfish desires that spring from sin; yet it is fiercely opposed by inspiration. See for yourself:

> There is not a point that needs to be dwelt upon more earnestly, repeated more frequently, or established more firmly in the minds of all, than the impossibility of fallen man meriting anything by his own best good works. Salvation is through faith in Jesus Christ alone. . . .
>
> Let the subject be made distinct and plain that it is not possible to effect anything in our standing before God or in the gift of God to us through creature merit. Should faith and works purchase the gift of salvation for anyone, then the Creator is under obligation to the creature. Here is an opportunity for falsehood to be accepted as truth. If any man can merit salvation by anything he may do, then he is in the same position as the Catholic to do penance for his sins. Salvation, then, is partly of debt, that may be earned as wages. If man cannot, by any of his good works, merit salvation, then it must be wholly of grace, received by man as a sinner because he receives and believes in Jesus. It is wholly a free gift.[11]

It is one of the "doctrines of demons" (1 Timothy 4:1) and of the beast that a person can "merit salvation by anything he may do." The third angel counters, "For by grace you have been saved through faith, and that not of yourselves; it is the gift of God" (Ephesians 2:8). A gift is something we receive. We can't earn it. We cannot be good enough to merit it. We don't deserve it. Ellen White testified that this subject must be "made distinct and plain." Paul did just that when he wrote, "If [it is] by grace, then it is no longer of works; otherwise grace is no longer grace" (Romans 11:6). Just like a baby is born either a boy or a girl, so is salvation either by grace or works. "It can't be both!" Paul thundered.

> Forgiveness, reconciliation with God, comes to us, not as a reward for our works, it is not bestowed because of the merit of sinful men, but it is a gift unto us, having in the spotless righteousness of Christ its foundation for bestowal.[12]

The old hymn still rings true, "My hope is built on nothing less than Jesus' blood and righteousness. I dare not trust the sweetest frame, but wholly lean on Jesus' name." The world has its big names—Rush Limbaugh, Steven Spielberg, Tom Cruise, and Madonna. Tomorrow there will be others. But eternal life comes *only* "by the name of Jesus Christ of Nazareth. . . . Nor is there salvation in any other, for there is no other name under heaven given among men by which we must be saved" (Acts 4:10, 12).

To reach heaven, we *must* relearn our spiritual ABCs.

Only then can we ever hope to enjoy Graduation Day.

---

1. *1893 General Conference Bulletin,* 296.
2. E. J. Waggoner, *Signs of the Times,* November 30, 1891.
3. E. J. Waggoner, "No Justification by the Law," *Signs of the Times,* September 1, 1890.
4. *1888 Materials,* 374.
5. Ibid., 810.
6. Ibid., 165, 166.
7. E. J. Waggoner, *Signs of the Times,* September 2, 1886.
8. Waggoner, *Christ and His Righteousness,* 67.
9. *Seventh-day Adventist Bible Commentary* (Washington, DC: Review and Herald®, 1957), 7:294, 295.
10. Ibid., 294.
11. *1888 Materials,* 811, 812.
12. White, *Mount of Blessing,* 115, 116.

CHAPTER TEN

WHY TRUST IN FILTHY RAGS?

"I FOCUS ON THOSE WHO ARE GOOD AND SEEK TO EMULATE THEM,
AND FOCUS ON THOSE WHO ARE BAD IN ORDER TO BE REMINDED
OF WHAT NEEDS TO CHANGE IN MYSELF."
—Confucius (551–479 B.C.),
Chinese politician, editor, and social philosopher

A ll our righteousnesses are like filthy rags" (Isaiah 64:6). "There is none righteous, no, not one" (Romans 3:10). Why not? Because "Your righteousness is an everlasting righteousness, and Your law is truth" (Psalm 119:142). In order for a man to be truly righteous, he must obey God's righteous law throughout his entire life. Just as one ink stain on a white collar dirties the collar, even so will a single sin spoil righteousness. Now, each of us has many more spots than just one stain. Our lives have been submerged in ink. So how much righteousness do we have? Ellen White clarified this: "Since we are sinful, and unholy, we cannot obey the holy law. We have no righteousness of our own with which to meet the claims of law of God."[1] That little word "no" means none. Zero.

We often think our great need is for a larger bank account, a better job, a new car, a house, or some other thing. But our greatest need is for righteousness. Jesus said, "Seek first the kingdom of God and His righteousness" (Matthew 6:33). Notice carefully whose righteousness we are to seek. Our own? No. Jesus said, "*His* righteousness." The problem with ancient Israel was that "they being ignorant of God s righteousness" were continually "seeking to establish their own righteousness" (Romans 10:3).

This is natural to fallen human nature.

It is a dead end.

When I was a boy I heard the story of a little train rolling up a large mountain. Though the ascent was hard, the train kept saying to itself, "I think I can, I think I can, I think I can." After much strain and exertion, the train reached the top of the hill. Like that little train, we often try to reach heaven by our own efforts, while at the same time we try to cover up our past failures by rationalizing them away. Ultimately, we want to prove that we are worthy, have merit, and thus establish our own righteousness. But the Bible says that salvation is "not of works, lest anyone should boast" (Ephesians 2:9). Again, "Where is boasting then? It is excluded. By what law? Of works? No, but by the law of faith" (Romans 3:27).

Mark it well. These Scriptures reveal that seeking salvation by works is a pride endeavor. Think about it. If we could reach the top of the hill in our own strength, then we could boast, "I did it. Look at me!" Then, instead of saying, "How great Thou art," we'd say, "How great *I am.*" Thus we would be repeating the sin of Lucifer, who desired to be first in heaven and who wanted to take the place of God. (See Isaiah 14:12–14.) Thus the root problem with righteousness by works is not only that it simply doesn't work, but also that it is a subtle effort of self proudly striving to be its own god. Again, it is really the same selfish desire that—hiding behind a mask of self-goodness—began with the devil himself and is the "very root of all sins." Trying to become little gods is not only the foundation of the New Age movement but also the basis of the righteousness-by-works movement sometimes seen in the church.

At the 1893 General Conference Session, Elder A. T. Jones spent a great deal of time explaining the relationship between Satan, self, and righteousness by works. Speaking to the delegates, he said:

> We need not go back into the depths of Satan's experience; we all know what it was that caused his fall. What was that? [Congregation: 'Pride.'] But self was the root of the pride; self is the root of everything; pride is the fruit of self only.[2]

Jones continued, "Well, that is the mind that is in all mankind. Now let us see how this carnal mind, this natural man, works in the matter of righteousness, in the matter of justification."[3] Jones then explained that righteousness by works is utterly satanic. "It is simply the natural mind depending upon itself, working through itself, exalting itself; and then covering it all up with a profession of a belief in this, that, and the other, but having no power of God."[4]

Bringing his point home, he added, "What is the condition of that man then who begins to think himself pretty good? And praises himself? Satan's delusion is upon him."[5]

With the skill of a spider we often attempt to weave for ourselves a garment of righteousness, but what is actually produced is a web of self-righteousness with which we trap ourselves. Isaiah wrote, "Their webs will not become garments, nor will they cover themselves with their works; their works are works of iniquity" (Isaiah 59:6). Again, we cannot cover our guilt by rationalizing or by trying to be good, any more than Adam and Eve could cover their sin with fig leaves. And these very efforts, if motivated by a "selfish desire," are themselves "works of iniquity." Thus it is literally true that "all our righteousnesses are as filthy rags" (Isaiah 64:6). Don't miss this point. Self-righteousness is not real righteousness. Instead, it is sin, and "sin is lawlessness" (1 John 3:4). So, how much genuine righteousness do we sinners actually have? "We have no righteousness with which to meet the claims of the law of God."[6]

Don't forget it. *None.*

In the famous tale of the emperor's new clothes, a crafty merchant tricked the king into believing that an invisible garment that didn't exist was really there. "Only the ignorant can't see it," he was told. The king's eyes were finally opened on the day of a parade when a little boy in the crowd shouted, "Daddy, the king is naked!" Millions today have also been tricked by the sneaky serpent into believing that their flimsy garments of self-righteousness will stand the test. But in the Day of Judgment, these spider webs and fig-leaf robes will prove to be non-existent. Realizing now that we are naked, our only hope is in being clothed with the real robe of the righteousness of Jesus Christ.

This is especially true for those who flatter themselves that they are "good people." Good people? How good? Not good enough!

We may have flattered ourselves, as did Nicodemus, that our life has been upright, that our moral character is correct, and think that we need not humble the heart before God, like the common sinner: but when the light from Christ shines into our souls, we shall see how impure we are; we shall discern the selfishness of motive, the enmity against God, that has defiled every act of life. Then we shall know that our own righteousness is indeed as filthy rags, and that the blood of Christ alone can cleanse us from the defilement of sin, and renew our hearts in His own likeness.

One ray of the glory of God, one gleam of the purity of Christ, penetrating the soul, makes every spot of defilement painfully distinct, and lays bare the deformity and defects of the human character. It makes apparent the unhallowed desires, the infidelity of the heart, the impurity of the lips. The sinner's acts of disloyalty in making void the law of God, are exposed to his sight, and his spirit is stricken and afflicted under the searching influence of the Spirit of God. He loathes himself as he views the pure, spotless character of Christ. . . .

The soul thus touched will hate its selfishness, abhor its self-love, and will seek, through Christ's righteousness, for the purity of heart that is in harmony with the law of God and the character of Christ.[7]

The true teaching of the third angel's message warns us not to be deceived by "invisible garments." Trying to weave them about ourselves is not only a waste of time but it could cost us our souls.

Don't be duped by crafty merchants.

Trust the King.

---

1. White, *Steps to Christ,* 62.
2. 1893 *General Conference Bulletin,* 257.
3. Ibid., 260.
4. Ibid., 265.
5. Ibid., 345.
6. White, *Steps to Christ,* 62.
7. Ibid., 28, 29.

CHAPTER ELEVEN

JESUS CHRIST IS OUR RIGHTEOUSNESS

"EVERYTHING IN CHRIST ASTONISHES ME. HIS SPIRIT OVERAWES ME,
AND HIS WILL CONFOUNDS ME. BETWEEN HIM AND WHOEVER ELSE
IN THE WORLD THERE IS NO POSSIBLE TERM OF COMPARISON. HE IS
TRULY A BEING BY HIMSELF."
—Napoleon Bonaparte (1769–1821), military general and emperor of France

An ancient prophecy about Jesus Christ reveals, "This is His name by which He will be called: the Lord our righteousness" (Jeremiah 23:6). Ellen White said to the delegates at the Minneapolis Conference, "I see the beauty of the truth in the presentation of the righteousness of Christ in relation to the law as the Doctor [E. J. Waggoner] has placed it before us."[1] We have been informed that during the closing hours of history, "One interest will prevail, one subject will swallow up every other,—Christ our Righteousness."[2]

The Holy Scriptures informs us of a garment that is far different from the deceived emperor's invisible clothes. It's not just a robe but the robe, and it's real. Notice carefully. Isaiah rejoiced, "He has covered me with the robe of righteousness" (Isaiah 61:10). Addressing the Laodicean church, the True Witness pleads, "Buy from Me . . . white garments, that you may be clothed, that the shame of your nakedness may not be revealed" (Revelation 3:18). Those who receive this spotless robe are ready for Armageddon. " 'Behold, I am coming as a thief. Blessed is he who watches, and keeps his garments, lest he walk naked and they see his shame.' And they gathered them together to the place called in Hebrew, Armageddon" (Revelation 16:15, 16).

It's time to carefully unlock the true meaning of the mysterious phrase, "Christ our Righteousness." What exactly is "the robe of righteousness" that Isaiah wrote about, with which God covers His people before Armageddon? And what is "the righteousness of Christ in relation to the law"[3] that E. J. Waggoner preached about at Minneapolis?

To begin with, we have already established from both the Bible and Ellen White's writings that "righteousness is defined by the standard of God's holy law, as expressed in the ten precepts given on Sinai"[4] (see Psalm 119:172; Romans 9:31). Therefore the expressions "Christ our Righteousness" and "the robe of righteousness" must have something to do with Jesus Himself and His perfect obedience to the Ten Commandments in our behalf.

Jesus told a parable about "a certain king who arranged a marriage for his son" (Matthew 22:2). Once everything was prepared, the king not only invited his subjects to "come to the wedding" (verse 4) but also graciously provided a special wedding garment for each guest. Unfortunately, one poor soul neglected to wear it when he entered the palace. He "did not have on a wedding garment" (verse 11). Could he remain inside the royal residence? No. To the man's horror, the king then instructed his servants to cast the poor fellow "into outer darkness" (verse 13). In her chapter, "Without a Wedding Garment," Ellen White commented:

> The white robe of innocence was worn by our first parents when they were placed in holy Eden. They lived in perfect conformity to the will of God. All the strength of their affections was given to their heavenly Father. A beautiful soft light, the light of God, enshrouded the holy pair. This robe of light was a symbol of their spiritual garments of heavenly innocence. Had they remained true to God it would ever have continued to enshroud them. But when sin entered, they severed their connection with God, and the light that had encircled them departed. Naked and ashamed, they tried to supply the place of the heavenly garments by sewing together fig leaves for a covering. . . .
>
> This is what transgressors of God's law have done ever since the day of Adam and Eve's disobedience. They have sewed together fig leaves to cover the nakedness caused by transgression. They have worn the garments of their own devising, by their works they have tried to cover their sins, and make themselves acceptable with God. But this they can never do. Nothing can man devise to supply the place of his lost robe of innocence. No fig leaf garment, no worldly citizen dress, can be worn by those who sit down with Christ and angels at the marriage supper of the Lamb.
>
> Only the covering which Christ Himself has provided can make us

meet to appear in God's presence. This covering, the robe of His own righteousness, Christ will put upon every repenting, believing soul. "I counsel thee," He says, "to buy of Me . . . white raiment, that thou mayest be clothed, and that the shame of thy nakedness do not appear" (Revelation 3:18). This robe, woven in the loom of heaven, has in it not one thread of human devising. Christ in His humanity wrought out a perfect character . . . Christ was obedient to every requirement of the law.[5]

A. T. Jones read these paragraphs and was deeply moved. Five years after the Minneapolis conference, he was one of the speakers at the 1893 General Conference Session. Addressing the delegates, Jones commented:

You remember the description that we already have of that raiment. The figure is, it is, "that garment that was woven in the loom of heaven, in which there is not a single thread of human making." Brethren, that garment was woven in a human body—the flesh of Christ—was the loom, was it not? That garment was woven in Jesus; in the same flesh that you and I have . . . for He took part of the same flesh and blood that we have. . . . What was it that was made there? [Voice: "The garment of righteousness."] And it is for all of us. The righteousness of Christ—the life that He lived—for you and for me, that is, we are considering to-night, that is the garment.[6]

Nearly two thousand years ago our heavenly Father looked down from His royal throne upon the helpless human family. With infinite discernment, He saw that "we have no righteousness of our own with which to meet the claims of the law of God."[7] Yet He loved us still! Moved by incomprehensible compassion, and at a cost we can never fully appreciate, He sent "His only begotten Son" to planet Earth to become human and to keep the Ten Commandments in our behalf. "The Word became flesh," wrote John, "and dwelt among us" (John 1:14). "Inasmuch then as the children have partaken of flesh and blood, He Himself likewise shared in the same" (Hebrews 2:14). Made "in the likeness of sinful flesh," Jesus Christ, the God-Man, was in "all points tempted like as we are, yet without sin" (Romans 8:3; Hebrews 4:15).

For thirty-three years our Savior obeyed the Ten Commandments and revealed the gracious character of our loving God. As a twelve-year-old, the New Testament reports, Jesus honored His father and mother. "He [Jesus] went down with them [Joseph and Mary] and came to Nazareth, and was subject to them" (Luke 2:51). He obeyed the fifth commandment (Exodus 20:12) *in our behalf.* After His baptism, when tempted in the wilderness by the devil, Jesus said to the enemy, " 'Get behind Me, Satan! For it is written, "You shall worship the Lord your God, and Him only you shall serve." ' " (Luke 4:8). Here Christ kept the first commandment (Exodus 20:3) *in our behalf.* At the beginning of His public ministry, "as His custom was, He went into the synagogue on the Sabbath day" (Luke 4:16). Thus He obeyed the fourth commandment (Exodus 20:8–11) also *in our behalf.* He obeyed all ten, all the time, without any ink spots.

Throughout His entire earthly pilgrimage, day by day, moment by moment, Jesus kept the law of God. Was it easy? Hardly. Satan threw every weapon from hell against Christ to lead Him into some sin. Just one. The intensity of the conflict was greater than World War I, World War II, Vietnam, or any Gulf war. What were the stakes? For Jesus, it was not only the honor of God and the salvation of sinners but also the eternal security of the universe itself. For Satan, it was his own existence. Yet "there was in Him nothing that responded to Satan's sophistry. He did not consent to sin. Not even by a thought did He yield to temptation."[8] Even the "selfish desire" which lies at "the very root of all sins" found no place in the loving heart of the Sinless One. "In the Savior's life the principles of God's law—love to God and man—were perfectly exemplified. Benevolence, unselfish love, was the life of His soul."[9]

As a human being, Jesus "learned obedience by the things which He suffered" (Hebrews 5:8). Through constant surrender and daily faith in the power of God, He was able to testify at the end of His life, "I have kept My Father's commandments." "I have finished the work which You have given Me to do" (John 15:10; 17:4). Choice by choice, in the flesh, Jesus Christ wove in His own life a robe of righteous obedience to the Big Ten. And again, why did He do it? For us. This is why the holy prophecy predicted that someday His special name would be "THE LORD OUR RIGHTEOUSNESS" (Jeremiah 23:6). Today, He is "Jesus Christ the righteous" (1 John 2:2). He is Jesus, who is "wisdom from God—and righteousness and sanctification and redemption" (1 Corinthians 1:30). And thus, although unknown to most, the robe of Christ's righteousness is now "the richest gift that can be given to mortal man."[10] And the good news is that God Himself longs to give that robe to you and me.

What a wonderful Savior we have!

Paul wrote: "But now the righteousness of God apart from the law is revealed, being witnessed by the Law and the Prophets" (Romans 3:21). What does this mean? In 1890, with crystal clarity, E. J. Waggoner commented upon this exact scripture in the *Signs:*

"But now the righteousness of God apart from the law is manifested." . . . Well, since we can't get anything from the law itself, we shall have to get it apart from the law if we have any at all. But don't be alarmed, for remember that this righteousness which we are to get without or apart from the law, is "the righteousness of God." Why, that's just what the law is! Exactly; there can be no real righteousness which is not the righteousness of God, and all that righteousness is set forth in His law. We are going to have this righteousness which the law requires, yet not out of the law. . . . If we get the righteousness of God through Jesus Christ, it is evident that we have the righteousness which the law requires.[11]

Two weeks later, Waggoner penned this:

The law is the perfect pattern of truth, therefore it must declare all men guilty and not righteous; and no one can hope to atone for his guilt by deeds of righteousness, because his best efforts come far short of the required standard, and so really add to the measure of his guilt. In this extremity the righteousness of God, without the law, in the person of Jesus Christ is manifested. This righteousness is just that which the law demands.[12]

Essentially, the Ten Commandment law looks at Jesus Christ and "witnesses" to His righteousness. If the law could speak, it would say, "Ah, there is Jesus Christ the Man. There is the righteousness I am looking for." At the 1893 General Conference Session, Jones echoed Waggoner's words before an increasingly animated audience:

When the law finds us, does it want anything from us? [Congregation: "It wants righteousness."] What kind? [Congregation: "Perfect righteousness."] Whose? [Congregation: "God's."] God's righteousness? [Congregation: "Yes."]. . . . Will the law be content with anything less than that from you and from me? Will it accept anything less than that, a hair's breadth less? [Congregation: "No."] If we could come within a hair's breadth of it—that's too far short; we miss it. . . . "Well," says one, "I have not got it; I have done my best." But the law will say, "That is not what I want. I don't want your best; I want perfection. It is not your doing I want anyhow, it is God's I want: it is not your righteousness I am after."

That is what the law says to every man. Then when I am shut off thus at the very first question, and even then when I said I did my best, then I have nothing more to say. Is that not what the Scripture says: "That every mouth is stopped." It does just that, does it not? . . . But there comes a still, small voice saying, "Here is a perfect life." . . .

Where does that voice come from? [Congregation: "Christ."] Ah, the Lord Jesus Christ, who came and stood where I stand, in the flesh which I live; he lived there. . . . Well then, he simply comes and tells me: "Here, take this." That will satisfy, then, will it? [Congregation: "Yes."] The life manifested in Jesus Christ; that will satisfy the law. . . . Well then, is that not what the law wants all the time? It is Jesus Christ that the law wants.[13]

What precious information! Now we can understand more clearly why Ellen White, after hearing Waggoner's lectures in 1888 at Minneapolis, enthusiastically wrote: "I see the beauty of the truth in the presentation of the righteousness of Christ in relation to the law as the Doctor [E. J. Waggoner] has placed it before us."[14]

Here is a brief summary of Waggoner's essential points:

1. The Ten Commandments, because they are a perfect expression of the character of a righteous God, require righteousness from us.

2. But we have *no* righteousness of our own with which to meet the holy standard.

3. Jesus Christ kept the law perfectly in our behalf and has earned the royal right to become "The Lord our Righteousness."

4. Christ's own righteousness perfectly satisfies the law.

Jesus did all this because He loves us. His character is love, and His law of Ten Commandments is a written expression of His love. While on earth, and in response to man's sin, Jesus perfectly lived out as a human being the principles of His own law by unselfishly developing a righteous character in our behalf. Correctly combining together the pieces—law, love, God's character, His righteousness, and what Jesus accomplished—Ellen White penned these memorable words:

Righteousness is holiness, likeness to God, and "God is love" (1 John 4:16). It is conformity to the law of God, for "all Thy commandments are righteousness" (Psalm 119:172), and "love is the fulfilling of the law" (Romans 13:10). Righteousness is love, and love is the light and the life of God.

Then she added:

"The righteousness of God is embodied in Christ."

Then finally:

"We receive righteousness by receiving Him."[15]

Jesus Christ is the center of our salvation. He's it. In today's vernacular, "He's the real thing."

---

1. *1888 Materials*, 164.
2. *Review and Herald Extra*, December 23, 1890.
3. *1888 Materials*, 164.
4. White, *Steps to Christ*, 61.
5. White, *Christ's Object Lessons*, 310–312.
6. *1893 General Conference Bulletin*, 207.
7. White, *Steps to Christ*, 62.
8. White, *The Desire of Ages*, 123.
9. White, *Steps to Christ*, 28.
10. White, *Gospel Workers*, 349.
11. *Signs of the Times*, September 8, 1890.
12. *Signs of the Times*, September 22, 1890.
13. *1893 General Conference Bulletin*, 412.
14. *1888 Materials*, 164.
15. White, *Mount of Blessing*, 18.

CHAPTER TWELVE

A.D. 31—THE COSMIC CENTER

"WE BELIEVE THAT THE HISTORY OF THE WORLD IS BUT THE HISTORY
OF HIS INFLUENCE, AND THAT THE CENTRE OF THE WHOLE UNI-
VERSE IS THE CROSS OF CALVARY."
—Alexander Maclaren (1826–1910), notable British preacher

A December 11, 1994 article in *U.S. News & World Report* reported concerning the year 2000, "There is a broad expectation that 'when the
world's odometer ticks over to three zeros, it will have cosmic significance.' "[1]
Our generation is fascinated by the cosmos. Movies like *E.T., Starman,* and
Star Wars have captured the interest of millions. Yet the greatest event ever
of cosmic significance occurred in the year A.D. 31, when a heavenly Man
shouted, " 'It is finished' " (John 19:30) just before dying on a cross. Although
unseen by most of humanity, His supreme act of self-sacrifice captured the
attention of billions of holy angels who have no interest in Hollywood films.

What happened in A.D. 31 is the center of God's last message to the world.

In order for the plan of salvation to be carried out, Jesus Christ had to do
more than develop a righteous character by keeping the Ten Commandments
in our behalf. He also had to "give His life a ransom for many" (Mark 10:45).
In her significant article, "Looking Back at Minneapolis," Ellen White testified,

> When I stated before my brethren that I had heard for the first time
> the views of Elder E. J. Waggoner, some did not believe me. I stated that
> I had heard precious truths uttered that I could respond to with all my
> heart, for had not these great and glorious truths, the righteousness of
> Christ and the entire sacrifice made in behalf of man, been imprinted

indelibly on my mind by the Spirit of God?[2]

"Indelibly" means permanently. It can never be removed.

At Minneapolis, "the Lord in His great mercy sent a most precious message to His people through Elders Waggoner and Jones. This message was to bring more prominently before the world the uplifted Savior, the sacrifice for the sins of the whole world."[3] Today, more than 120 years later, Heaven's holiest efforts are still being energized by the challenge of lifting up the cross "more prominently." What else can turn the attention of baby boomers, baby busters, gen-Xers, and today's high-tech teenagers away from fantasy to reality?

It's time to define the gospel. Compelled by the Holy Spirit, Paul wrote,

> Moreover, brethren, I declare to you the gospel which I preached to you, which also you received and in which you stand, by which also you are saved, if you hold fast that word which I preached to you—unless you believed in vain.
>
> For I delivered to you first of all that which I also received: that Christ died for our sins according to the Scriptures (1 Corinthians 15:1–3).

Here is the gospel, pure and simple. It is the Good News that, outside Jerusalem, "Christ died for our sins according to the Scriptures, and that He was buried, and that He rose again the third day according to the Scriptures" (1 Corinthians 15:3, 4). Again, Christ "gave Himself for our sins" (Galatians 1:4). What is sin? "Sin is lawlessness" (1 John 3:4), says the Lord.

Therefore the gospel is the good news that Jesus Christ has already died for our sins of breaking the Ten Commandments. You may forget someone's name, or an appointment, or where you placed your car keys, but don't ever forget this. The salvation of your soul depends upon it.

We must be exceedingly careful not to be hoodwinked into believing "a different gospel, which is not another" (Galatians 1:6, 7). Paul felt so passionately about this that he warned about those who "pervert the gospel of Christ" or "preach any other gospel" (Galatians 1:7, 8). He even said that those who do this are in grave danger of ending up "accursed" (verse 9). Ellen White said simply, "Calvary stands as a memorial of the amazing sacrifice required to atone for the transgression of the divine law."[4] On Mount Sinai the Lord revealed Himself to Moses as

> "the LORD, the LORD God, merciful and gracious, longsuffering, and abounding in goodness and truth, keeping mercy for thousands, forgiving iniquity and transgression and sin, by no means clearing the guilty,

visiting the iniquity of the fathers upon the children and the children's children to the third and the fourth generation" (Exodus 34:6, 7).

Here the true character of God is described as a blend of mercy and justice. Moses didn't resist this revelation. He didn't try to make God merciful only, and not just. Rather, "Moses made haste and bowed his head toward the earth, and worshiped" (Exodus 34:8). Soon all the saved will sing "the song of Moses, the servant of God, and the song of the Lamb, saying: 'Great and marvelous are Your works, Lord God Almighty! Just and true are Your ways, O King of the saints!' " (Revelation 15:3).

If a man commits a serious crime against the just laws of an earthly government, justice requires that a penalty be executed. The Law of God is "holy and just and good" (Romans 7:12), the foundation of His government in heaven and in earth. Whenever any created being commits the heinous crime of breaking any one of the Ten Commandments, the justice of God also requires that a penalty be executed. What is the penalty? "The wages of sin is death" (Romans 6:23). "Wages" are not simply "natural consequences." If you have a job, your paycheck doesn't fall naturally into your pocket. It must be deliberately given to you by your employer. The same is true of "the wages of sin." They will be directly meted out by a just Judge to lost souls at the end of the millennium. The Lord will "render to each one according to his deeds" (Romans 2:6). " 'I will repay,' says the Lord" (Hebrews 10:30). In this life we do experience the natural consequences of countless evils; but this is not "the wages of sin." So far, there is only One who has ever fully experienced those wages; and that Person was Jesus Christ. Two years after the Minneapolis conference, E. J. Waggoner wrote an article in *Signs* entitled, "The Penalty of the Law." He stated the shocking truth,

If Adam had suffered the penalty of the law, he would have died an eternal death; for 'the wages of sin is death.' This means death simple and absolute, with no hope of a resurrection. The penalty of the law has fallen upon only one being, and that was Christ.[5]

Ellen White agreed.

The penalty must be exacted. The Lord does not save sinners by abolishing His law, the foundation of His government in heaven and in earth. The punishment has been endured by the sinner's substitute. Not that God is cruel and merciless, and Christ so merciful. . . . In the councils of heaven, before the world was created, the Father and the Son covenanted together that if man proved disloyal to God, Christ, one with the Father, would take the place of the transgressor, and suffer the penalty of justice that must fall upon him.[6]

Before entering Gethsemane, Jesus spoke these mysterious words to His disciples: " 'All of you will be made to stumble because of Me this night, for it is written: "I will strike the Shepherd, and the sheep of the flock will be scattered" ' " (Matthew 26:31). When Jesus said "it is written," He was referring to Zechariah 13:7. Commenting on this exact verse, Ellen White wrote:

> His suffering can best be described in the words of the prophet, "Awake, O sword, against My shepherd, and against the man that is My fellow, saith the Lord of hosts." Zechariah 13:7. As the substitute and surety for sinful man, Christ was suffering under divine justice. He saw what justice meant.[7]

The sword in Zechariah 13:7 was not the sword of injustice wielded by Judas, the Jewish Sanhedrin, Pontius Pilate, or Roman soldiers. No, instead, "the sword of justice was now to awake against God's dear Son."[8] Because of the entrance of sin into Adam and Eve in the Garden of Eden, heaven's Lamb was about to suffer in another garden outside Jerusalem. The penalty for breaking the Ten Commandments proclaimed on Mount Sinai was to fall with crushing force on Calvary. The same hand that wrote the law on stone would be nailed to a cross. As it is written, "Christ has redeemed us from the curse of the law, having become a curse for us" (Galatians 3:13). "The death of Christ proclaimed the justice of His Father's law in punishing the transgressor, in that He consented to suffer the penalty of the law Himself in order to save fallen man from its curse."[9] "He was paying the just claims of God's holy law."[10] Yes, a broken law crushed the cross. This is not fantasy but intense reality. Our mouths are "stopped" (Romans 3:19) as we begin to comprehend why our Savior had to die.

"Then Jesus came with them to a place called Gethsemane, and said to the disciples, 'Sit here while I go and pray over there' " (Matthew 26:36). As Jesus staggered into the Garden of Gethsemane with His disciples on that fateful Thursday evening, He became sorrowful and deeply distressed. Then He said to them, "My soul is exceedingly sorrowful, even to death. Stay here and watch with Me." He went a little farther and fell on His face, and prayed, saying, "O My Father, if it is possible, let this cup pass from Me; nevertheless, not as I will, but as You will" (Matthew 26:38).

Gethsemane is an olive garden east of Jerusalem. I visited there in 1983. The word *Gethsemane* literally means "oil press." On that fearful night, the "oil" of Christ's life was "pressed out" as the sins of the world pressed into His soul. As He prayed, His face was an inch from the dirt.

What we are about to contemplate changed my life nearly thirty years ago. In 1979, in a dormitory room at a state college in Southern California, I read "Gethsemane," a chapter in Ellen White's classic book, *The Desire of Ages*. I have never been the same since. Through that chapter, the Spirit of God finally reached me. It was this exact revelation of Jesus' love and suffering that delivered me from an aimless life mesmerized by rock music, alcohol, marijuana, cocaine, and LSD. In a few short weeks, my college major shifted from marketing to ministry. I don't think anything else could have done it. The realization that Christ's agony was because of my very own sins broke down every barrier. Truly the gospel is "the power of God to salvation for everyone who believes" (Romans 1:16).

I suggest you carefully and prayerfully read in your own Bible the entire chapters of Matthew 26 and 27. As you do, you will gain a deeper appreciation for what the Son of God did for you. Jesus loves you more than you can possibly know. Honestly, I believe it is not an accident that you are reading this book. God's providence has led you to this moment. Yes, right now. It's time for the "odometer" of your life to click over to A.D. 31, and for the Spirit of God to reach your heart. As you read through the following sacred section, let the Holy Spirit impress you with the infinite love of *your Savior*. He suffered for you—all for you. You might even want to stop reading for a moment, bow your head, and say a prayer.

The Bible says,

> He was wounded for our transgressions,
> He was bruised for our iniquities;
> The chastisement for our peace was upon Him,
> And by His stripes we are healed.
> All we like sheep have gone astray;
> We have turned, every one, to his own way;
> And the Lord has laid on Him the iniquity of us all (Isaiah 53:5, 6).

More than a hundred years ago, Ellen White penned the following inspiring paragraphs. This section is a bit lengthy, but who can measure its worth?

> In company with His disciples, the Saviour slowly made His way to the garden of Gethsemane. The Passover moon, broad and full, shone from a cloudless sky. The city of pilgrims' tents was hushed into silence.
>
> Jesus had been earnestly conversing with His disciples and instructing them; but as He neared Gethsemane, He became strangely silent. He had often visited this spot for meditation and prayer; but never with a heart so full of sorrow as upon this night of His last agony.

Throughout His life on earth He had walked in the light of God's presence. When in conflict with men who were inspired by the very spirit of Satan, He could say, "He that sent Me is with Me: the Father hath not left Me alone; for I do always those things that please Him." John 8:29. But now He seemed to be shut out from the light of God's sustaining presence. Now He was numbered with the transgressors. The guilt of fallen humanity He must bear. Upon Him who knew no sin must be laid the iniquity of us all. So dreadful does sin appear to Him, so great is the weight of guilt which He must bear, that He is tempted to fear it will shut Him out forever from His Father's love. Feeling how terrible is the wrath of God against transgression, He exclaims, "My soul is exceeding sorrowful, even unto death."

As they approached the garden, the disciples had marked the change that came over their Master. Never before had they seen Him so utterly sad and silent. As He proceeded, this strange sadness deepened; yet they dared not question Him as to the cause. His form swayed as if He were about to fall. Upon reaching the garden, the disciples looked anxiously for His usual place of retirement, that their Master might rest. Every step that He now took was with labored effort. He groaned aloud, as if suffering under the pressure of a terrible burden. Twice His companions supported Him, or He would have fallen to the earth.

Near the entrance to the garden, Jesus left all but three of the disciples, bidding them pray for themselves and for Him. With Peter, James, and John, He entered its secluded recesses. These three disciples were Christ's closest companions. They had beheld His glory on the mount of transfiguration; they had seen Moses and Elijah talking with Him; they had heard the voice from heaven; now in His great struggle, Christ desired their presence near Him. Often they had passed the night with Him in this retreat. On these occasions, after a season of watching and prayer, they would sleep undisturbed at a little distance from their Master, until He awoke them in the morning to go forth anew to labor. But now He desired them to spend the night with Him in prayer. Yet He could not bear that even they should witness the agony He was to endure. "Tarry ye here," He said, "and watch with Me."

He went a little distance from them—not so far but that they could both see and hear Him—and fell prostrate upon the ground. He felt that by sin He was being separated from His Father. The gulf was so broad, so black, so deep, that His spirit shuddered before it. This agony He must not exert His divine power to escape. As man He must suffer the consequences of man's sin. As man He must endure the wrath of God against transgression.

Christ was now standing in a different attitude from that in which He had ever stood before. His suffering can best be described in the words of the prophet, "Awake, O sword, against My shepherd, and against the man that is My fellow, saith the Lord of hosts." Zechariah 13:7. As the substitute and surety for sinful man, Christ was suffering under divine justice. He saw what justice meant. Hitherto He had been as an intercessor for others; now He longed to have an intercessor for Himself. As Christ felt His unity with the Father broken up, He feared that in His human nature He would be unable to endure the coming conflict with the powers of darkness. In the wilderness of temptation the destiny of the human race had been at stake. Christ was then conqueror. Now the tempter had come for the last fearful struggle. For this he had been preparing during the three years of Christ's ministry. Everything was at stake with him. If he failed here, his hope of mastery was lost; the kingdoms of the world would finally become Christ's; he himself would be overthrown and cast out. But if Christ could be overcome, the earth would become Satan's kingdom, and the human race would be forever in his power. With the issues of the conflict before Him, Christ's soul was filled with dread of separation from God. Satan told Him that if He became the surety for a sinful world, the separation would be eternal. He would be identified with Satan's kingdom, and would nevermore be one with God.

And what was to be gained by this sacrifice? How hopeless appeared the guilt and ingratitude of men! In its hardest features Satan pressed the situation upon the Redeemer: The people who claim to be above all others in temporal and spiritual advantages have rejected You. They are seeking to destroy You, the foundation, the center and seal of the promises made to them as a peculiar people. One of Your own disciples, who has listened to Your instruction, and has been among the foremost in church activities, will betray You. One of Your most zealous followers will deny You. All will forsake You. Christ's whole being abhorred the thought. That those whom He had undertaken to save, those whom He loved so much, should unite in the plots of Satan, this pierced His soul. The conflict was terrible. Its measure was the guilt of His nation, of His accusers and betrayer, the guilt of a world lying in wickedness. The sins of men weighed heavily upon Christ, and the sense of God's wrath against sin was crushing out His life.

Behold Him contemplating the price to be paid for the human soul. In His agony He clings to the cold ground, as if to prevent Himself from being drawn farther from God. The chilling dew of night falls upon His prostrate form, but He heeds it not. From His pale lips comes the bitter cry, "O My Father, if it be possible, let this cup pass from Me." Yet even now He adds, "Nevertheless not as I will, but as Thou wilt."[11]

Because God is just, He can "by no means [clear] the guilty" (Exodus 34:7). Yet because "God is love" (1 John 4:8), Jesus chose to "drink the cup apportioned to guilty man."[12]

The day that millions call Good Friday was a good day for us, but not for Jesus. At about 9:00 A.M., "they had come to a place called Golgotha, that is to say, Place of a Skull. . . . They crucified Him. . . . Sitting down, they kept watch over Him there. . . . Then two robbers were crucified with Him, one on the right and another on the left" (Matthew 27:33, 35, 36, 38). Spiked to a tree between two thieves, God's own Son hung suspended between heaven and earth. Before His crucifixion Jesus had told His disciples, " 'I say to you that this which is written must still be accomplished in Me: "And He was numbered with the transgressors." For the things concerning Me have an end.' " (Luke 22:37). That "end" had come. With nails in His hands and feet, with thorns pressed down upon His holy brow, our Savior suffered under the full weight of the curse of the broken law of God.

Consider carefully that there is much more to the cross than a Roman whip, nails, and thorns.

> Bodily pain was but a small part of the agony of God's dear Son. The sins of the world were upon Him, also the sense of His Father's wrath as He suffered the penalty of the law transgressed. It was these that crushed His divine soul. It was the hiding of His Father's face—a sense that His own dear Father had forsaken Him—which brought despair. The separation that sin makes between God and man was fully realized and keenly felt by the innocent, suffering Man of Calvary.[13]

When I was five years old my appendix ruptured, and I was rushed to a nearby hospital. Even at the age of fifty-four, I can still remember crying, screaming, and clinging to my dad as a doctor ripped me out of his arms toward the operating room. "Daddy, don't leave me!" I shouted hysterically. To no avail. I was separated from my father. Dear friend, so was Jesus on the cross. We can never fully appreciate the depth of horror that Christ felt when He finally cried out, "My God, My God, why have You forsaken Me?" (Matthew 27:46). There is no sentence ever spoken by human lips throughout world history as powerful as that one. Jesus and His Father were one from eternity. What caused their separation? Oh, it was sin . . . our sins of breaking the Ten Commandments. Because we broke the law, our sins broke His heart.

In a dream, a man saw Christ being scourged. The Roman tormentor flung the whip through the air into the innocent victim's back. Bits of pointed metal sank deep into His flesh. Finally the man could stand it no longer. Running forward, he yelled, "Stop!" But when he turned the Roman soldier around and saw his face, to his horror, he saw himself! Likewise, as we look at the cross, we see ourselves. We see what our sins have done to the Son of God.

Describing the epiphany of all ages, Ellen White wrote with an inspired pen,

> Upon Christ as our substitute and surety was laid the iniquity of us all. He was counted a transgressor, that He might redeem us from the condemnation of the law. The guilt of every descendant of Adam was pressing upon His heart. The wrath of God against sin, the terrible manifestation of His displeasure because of iniquity, filled the soul of His Son with consternation . . . with the weight of guilt He bears, He cannot see the Father's reconciling face. . . . He feared that sin was so offensive to God that Their separation was to be eternal. . . . It was the sense of sin, bringing the Father's wrath upon Him as man's substitute, that made the cup He drank so bitter, and broke the heart of the Son of God. . . . He, the Sin Bearer, endures the wrath of divine justice, and for thy sake becomes sin itself.[14]

Is there significance to Christ hanging on a tree? Yes. Paul wrote, "Christ has redeemed us from the curse of the law, having become a curse for us (for it is written, 'Cursed is everyone who hangs on a tree')" (Galatians 3:13). In Old Testament times, the corpses of the worst offenders against God were hung on trees. Moses wrote,

> If a man has committed a sin deserving of death, and he is put to death, and you hang him on a tree, his body shall not remain overnight on the tree, but you shall surely bury him that day, so that you do not defile the land which the Lord your God is giving you as an inheritance; for he who is hanged is accursed of God (Deuteronomy 21:22, 23).

The ultimate curse for breaking God's holy law is death. To pay the price, Jesus Christ actually became "accursed of God" when He hung upon the cross! Wonder, O heavens! Be astonished, O earth!

When God proclaimed His Law upon Sinai, "the whole mountain quaked greatly" (Exodus 19:18). At the exact moment when Jesus died, "the earth quaked, and the rocks were split" (Matthew 27:51). Then, for many moments there was silence. Billions of angels and unfallen beings hardly breathed. You could have heard a pin drop throughout the universe. The unthinkable had happened. Jesus Christ, the Creator of all life (see John 1:10) *was dead.* He hung motionless—silent on the cross. Then a shout rang out that will echo into eternity: "Now salvation, and strength, and the kingdom of our God, and the power of His Christ have come" (Revelation 12:10).

"By the grace of God" our Savior "taste[d] death for everyone" (Hebrews 2:9). We do not deserve this special treatment. We have done nothing to earn or merit it. In fact, we caused His death. And it has already been accomplished, even before we were born. Every breath we have ever taken, every bite of food, every good thing we have ever received or ever will receive, comes to us solely through the cross of Jesus Christ. Is this why Paul wrote, "Where is boasting then? It is excluded" (Romans 3:27). Is this why he testified, "God forbid that I should boast except in the cross of our Lord Jesus Christ, by whom the world has been crucified to me, and I to the world" (Galatians 6:14)? Is this why Ellen White so earnestly appealed that we "bring more prominently before the world the uplifted Savior, the sacrifice for the sins of the whole world"?[15]

YES, THIS IS THE REASON.

"But God demonstrates His own love toward us, in that while we were still sinners, Christ died for us" (Romans 5:8). While we didn't care. While we lived to please only ourselves. When the Bible and Christianity appeared irrelevant. When TV, sports, wild music, entertainment, money, passion, and worldly pleasures absorbed our attention. When anything and everything took the place of the Father, His Son, and His Holy Spirit inside our souls, "Christ died for us." Why? Why? Why? It *was love,* my friend. Unfathomable, unselfish love for you and for me. No words can fully express it. No book can really describe it. But our hearts can feel it, if we don't resist it.

The realization of this love is what compelled a young man in the 1800s named E. J. Waggoner to embark on his career as a preacher of the cross. At an outdoor camp meeting in California in 1882, he had a remarkable experience.

> Suddenly a light shone about me, and the tent seemed illumined, as though the sun were shining; I saw Christ crucified for me, and to me was revealed for the first time in my life the fact that God loved me and that Christ gave Himself for me personally. It was all for me.[16]

Dear friend, it was all for you. All your sins have already been paid for. The full penalty of divine justice has already fallen upon Jesus Christ. Meditate on this:

> Justice and Mercy stood apart, in opposition to each other, separated by a wide gulf. The Lord our Redeemer clothed His divinity with humanity, and wrought out in behalf of man a character that was

without spot or blemish. He planted His cross midway between heaven and earth, and made it the object of attraction which reached both ways, drawing both Justice and Mercy across the gulf. Justice moved from its exalted throne, and with all the armies of heaven approached the cross. There it saw One equal with God bearing the penalty for all injustice and sin. With perfect satisfaction Justice bowed in reverence at the cross, saying, "It is enough."[17]

In his monumental work, *Christ and His Righteousness,* published shortly after the Minneapolis conference, Waggoner later wrote:

He vindicates the integrity of His law, by submitting in His own Person to the penalty that was due the sinner. "But the innocent suffered for the guilty." True, but the innocent Sufferer "gave Himself voluntarily, in order that He might in justice to His government do what His love prompted, namely, pass by the injury done to Himself as the ruler of the universe."[18]

Ellen White added,

The salvation of man is accomplished at an infinite expense to heaven; the sacrifice made is equal to the broadest demands of the broken law of God.[19]

Alleluia! What happened in A.D. 31 outside the city of Jerusalem is infinitely more important than the events of A.D. 476 (when the Roman Empire collapsed), A.D. 1492 (when Columbus discovered America), and A.D. 2001 (when terrorists attacked the World Trade Center). What happened in A.D. 31 has become the center of the universe. It has "cosmic significance." It is also the center of the third angel's message. Within its depths is "the special power of the Holy Spirit." And to a world lost in sin, it is the center of God's last message to His world today. Because justice was fully satisfied on Calvary, the King of the universe can now "be just and the justifier of the one who has faith in Jesus" (Romans 3:26).

To this truth, we shall turn our attention next.

You'll love it.

---

1. Jeffery L. Sheler, Gareth G. Cook, and David Makovsky, "The Christmas Covenant," *US News & World Report,* posted December 11, 1994, http://www .usnews.com/usnews/culture/articles/941219/archive_012189.htm.

2. *1888 Materials,* 217.

3. White, *Testimonies to Ministers,* 91.

4. White, *Steps to Christ,* 33,

5. E. J. Waggoner, "The Penalty of the Law," *Signs of the Times,* Aug. 4, 1890.

6. *Seventh-day Adventist Bible Commentary,* 7A:294.

7. White, *The Desire of Ages,* 686.

8. White, *Testimonies for the Church,* 2:207.

9. Ibid., 201.

10. Ibid., 209.

11. White, *The Desire of Ages,* 685–687.

12. Ibid., 690.

13. White, *Testimonies for the Church,* 2:203.

14. White, *The Desire of Ages,* 753, 756.

15. White, *Testimonies to Ministers,* 91.

16. Clinton Wahlen, "What Did E. J. Waggoner Say at Minneapolis?" *Adventist Heritage* 13 (Winter 1988), 22.

17. *Seventh-day Adventist Bible Commentary,* 7A:294.

18. Waggoner, *Christ and His Righteousness,* 63.

19. White, *The Great Controversy,* 489.

CHAPTER THIRTEEN

COVERED AND COUNTED RIGHTEOUS

"WITHOUT FORGIVENESS, THERE IS NO FUTURE."
—Desmond Tutu (1931–),
South African retired Anglican bishop and social activist

W e conclude that a man is justified by faith apart from the deeds of the law" (Romans 3:28). "Having been justified by faith, we have peace with God through our Lord Jesus Christ" (Romans 5:1). On April 4, 1893, Ellen White's article titled, "Address to the Church," was published in the official Seventh-day Adventist paper, *The Review and Herald*. With enthusiasm she identified "the sweetest melodies that come from God through human lips" as "justification by faith, and the imputed righteousness of Christ."[1] This truth is infinitely more important than winning a high-dollar sweepstakes, a lottery, or a jackpot in Las Vegas. Such diversions only lead minds away from the true gold of the righteousness of Jesus Christ.

The biblical message of justification by faith is one of the most glorious and life-changing truths in God's Word. In "Looking Back at Minneapolis," Ellen White wrote,

Elder E. J. Waggoner had the privilege granted him of speaking plainly and presenting his views upon justification by faith and the righteousness of Christ in relation to the law. This was no new light, but it was old light placed where it should be in the third angel's message.[2]

As we have already seen, "justification" has special reference to our standing before God and His Ten Commandment law. Waggoner explained, "Justification has reference to the moral law. From the transgression of that man needs justification."[3] The Law of God is "just" (Romans 7:12). Before "the law . . . every mouth is stopped" and "all the world" stands "guilty before God" (Romans 3:19). To be justified simply means that we are no longer "guilty before God" because our sin and guiltiness has been mercifully removed from us. Now, when the Lord looks at us, He considers us "just," even though we have previously been Ten Commandment breakers. Ellen White describes it this way: "It is our privilege to go to Jesus and be cleansed, and to stand before the law without shame or remorse."[4] Because justice was satisfied on Calvary, God can "be just and the justifier of the one who has faith in Jesus" (Romans 3:26). "Glorious truth!—just to His own law, and yet the Justifier of all that believe in Jesus."[5] What could be more wonderful? And it is our privilege to experience this precious reality right now.

What about the other expression, "the imputed righteousness of Christ"? What does it mean? Ellen White wrote, "It was possible for Adam, before the fall, to form a righteous character by obedience to God's law. But he failed to do this."[6] But what Adam "failed" to do, Jesus flawlessly accomplished. He did "form a righteous character by obedience to God's law," and that "righteous character" is "the righteousness of Christ." Paul wrote of "the blessedness of the man to whom God imputes righteousness apart from works" (Romans 4:6). To "impute" means to credit. The Bible is saying that God will impute— credit and apply—"the righteousness of Christ" to our individual account in the books of heaven (see Daniel 7:10; Revelation 20:12). Then when God looks at our record, He not only sees our personal sins of breaking the Big Ten "covered," but also thirty-three years of the obedience of Jesus Christ in the place of those sins. This truth is part of the glory of the third angel's message.

Waggoner described it this way:

> Now God says that He will impute the righteousness of Christ to everyone who will fully believe on Him. Impute means "to set to the account of." Therefore we are to understand that whenever we accept Christ, His righteousness is set to our account. Thus "the righteousness of God" is manifested in our past lives, even though we ourselves have never done a single act of righteousness. So, we have the wonder of perfect obedience to the law, without a single righteous act on our part. The righteousness of God without the law—Christ's righteousness imputed to us.[7]

Ellen White agreed: "The righteousness of Christ is placed on the debtor's account, and against his name on the balance sheet is written, Pardoned. Eternal Life."[8] "The Lord imputes to the believer the righteousness of Christ, and pronounces him righteous before the universe."[9]

How's this for a message of "cosmic significance"?

This is "the truth of the gospel" (Galatians 2:5). As a "great light" with "the special power of the Holy Spirit" it burst upon the delegates at Minneapolis. "The Sun of Righteousness" began to shine through the dark clouds of unbelief "with healing in His wings" (Malachi 4:2). Filled with love for Jesus, Ellen White responded,

> I see the beauty of the truth in the presentation of the righteousness of Christ in relation to the law as the Doctor [E. J. Waggoner] has placed it before us. You say, many of you, it is light and truth. Yet you have not presented it in this light heretofore.[10]

"In Minneapolis God gave precious gems of truth to His people in new settings."[11] Yes, it was new. It was biblical. It was powerful. It was "the beginning of the light of the angel whose glory shall fill the whole earth."[12]

But there was someone lurking in the shadows of Minneapolis who wasn't pleased at all. It was Satan himself. His mighty angelic form trembled for his own existence. He counseled with his angels. They all knew that if this message were not stopped, it would be D-Day for the kingdom of darkness. They all realized that for sinful mortals:

> The thought that the righteousness of Christ is imputed to us, not because of any merit on our part, but as a free gift from God, is a precious thought. The enemy of God and man is not willing that this truth should be clearly presented; for he knows that if the people receive it fully, his power will be broken.[13]

Believe me, Satan's hosts don't want their power broken!

Think about it. If you were downcast, discouraged, or depressed, and someone offered you a billion dollars tax free, with no strings attached, would that have any effect on your mood? No doubt. Now, if God Himself applied to your personal account in heaven thirty-three years of the righteousness of Jesus Christ and then publicly pronounced you righteous before the universe—would this empower your Christian life? Would such a revelation of indescribable love help uproot that "very root of all sins, the selfish desire, from which springs the sinful act"[14]? Would it help detoxify your soul of any lingering "sympathy for the devil" (the title of a popular rock song)?

As we near "the great day of the LORD" (Zephaniah 1:14), it is still God's plan that "this truth" should supply "the special power of the Holy Spirit" to enable us to make a break with Satan's legions and to carry "the truth to the world, as the apostles proclaimed it after the day of Pentecost."[15]

Is it not high time for Pentecost II?

If not now, when? If not us, then who?

May God help us!

From New Zealand, in 1893, Ellen White wrote to A. T. Jones to clarify a vital point: "There are conditions to our receiving justification and sanctification and the righteousness of Christ."[16] Really? Indeed. But this need not discourage us at all. Why not? Because "the conditions of obtaining mercy of God are simple and just and reasonable."[17] In his greatest epistle, Paul also clarified that "the righteousness of God" comes "through faith in Jesus Christ" (Romans 3:22). Look closely: God can be "just and the justifier of the one who has faith in Jesus" (Romans 3:26). "Therefore being justified by faith, we have peace with God through our Lord Jesus Christ" (Romans 5:1). With faith as a condition, instead of discouraging us, this should make us very happy.

Two years after the Minneapolis Conference, Ellen White specified exactly how anyone who really wants to could meet this "simple, just, and reasonable" condition of God:

> Righteousness is obedience to the law. The law demands righteousness, and this the sinner owes to the law; but he is incapable of rendering it. The only way in which he may attain to righteousness is by faith. By faith he can bring to God the merits of Christ, and the Lord places the obedience of His Son to the sinner's account. Christ's righteousness is accepted in place of man's failure, and God receives, pardons, justifies, the repentant, believing soul, treats him as though he were righteous, and loves him as He loves His Son. This is how faith is accounted righteousness.[18]

When we pray, we must be simple enough to "by faith bring to God the merits of Christ." Like a little child we can say, "Father, here are the merits of Jesus." If we are willing to do it this way, then the Lord Jesus Himself will make sure we are justified. If we are not simple enough, then we will miss it entirely. Jesus said, "Whoever does not receive the kingdom of God as a little child will by no means enter it" (Luke 18:17). We can do it and then trust the Lord that it is done, that we have received a "full and complete pardon for sin."

Again, "Faith is the only condition upon which justification can be obtained, and faith includes not only belief but trust."[19] Yes, we must trust the hand that was nailed to the cross for us. Paul wrote, "Faith comes by hearing, and hearing by the word of God" (Romans 10:17). God's word produces faith.

As we have heard the message of the love and suffering of Jesus for us, has not this produced enough faith in our hearts with which to trust Him? Jesus said, "Let not your heart be troubled; you believe in God, believe also in Me" (John 14:1). John also wrote, "He who believes in Him is not condemned" (John 3:18). Remember, justification is the opposite of condemnation.

I once saw a cartoon in a newspaper picturing a man hanging on a tree limb over a cliff. As the limb began to crack, he shouted into the heavens, "Is anyone up there? Help!"

The voice of God came down from the sky saying, "I'm here!"

The hanging man asked, "What shall I do?"

God responded, "Just let go. My hands are beneath you. Trust Me."

The hanging man thought for a moment. In the last frame of the cartoon he shouted back up into the sky, "Is there anyone else up there?"

This poor soul lacked faith. The Bible says, "With God nothing will be impossible" (Luke 1:37). If we will but trust the Lord Jesus Christ, He will surely clothe us with the white robe of His righteousness. Oh, how He longs to clothe each one of us!

Now notice another key point: in order to show his faith, the man in the cartoon needed to let go of the limb. The same is true for us. We also must be willing to let go of our sins. The Bible speaks so simply about the condition and promise. It is written, "If we confess our sins, He is faithful and just to forgive us our sins and to cleanse us from all unrighteousness" (1 John 1:9). Sadly,

> Here is where thousands fail; they do not believe that Jesus pardons them personally, individually. They do not take God at His word. It is the privilege of all who comply with the conditions to know for themselves that pardon is freely extended for every sin. Put away the suspicion that God's promises are not meant for you. They are for every repentant transgressor.[20]

Yes, God's promises are for you. Jesus loves you. He died that you might be forgiven. He, your sin-pardoning Savior, longs for you to come home.

A young reckless teenager once had a terrible argument with his dad. His last words were "I'm leaving. You will never see me again!" as he stormed out of the house. He thought he could make it on his own. But after three difficult years, remorseful thoughts turned him toward home. *Will my father take me back?* he wondered. He finally gathered the courage to phone his mother. "Mom, please talk to Dad. Tell him I will be passing by the foot of our hill on a train next Monday afternoon. Ask him to hang something white on the porch it he wants me back. If I see anything white, I'll come home."

Then he hung up.

On that Monday morning, a fearful teenager boarded the train and happened to sit next to a minister. "Why are you so nervous?" the man asked.

The boy told him the whole story. "Mister," he said, "when we roll around the curve ahead, will you look out the window at the house on the top of the hill? If you see anything white, tell me. I'm scared to look!"

As the train rounded the last bend and the minister looked through the glass, the sight caused him to forget his ministerial dignity. Jumping to his feet, the pastor shouted, "Look, son. Look!"

Fearfully opening his eyes, the boy saw his little house on the hill completely covered with every white sheet, white blanket, white bedspread, white towel, white tablecloth, white napkin, and white handkerchief that his parents owned. Oh, how they wanted him home. The last thing the minister saw of the boy was the back of his legs running as fast as possible up the hill, across the porch, through the white sheets, and into the waiting arms of his lonely parents.

Oh friend, does Jesus want you to come home too? If you only knew how much! Will you not respond to His drawing by making a decision to leave "the far country" and return to your Father's house? If you do, He will definitely forgive you. More than this, He will command His servants to "bring out the best robe and put it on" you (Luke 15:22). The "best robe" is nothing other than the pure white robe of the righteousness of Jesus Christ. Yes, Jesus does love you, and He wants you home. Your Savior will say, "Take away the filthy garments from him . . . I will clothe you with rich robes" (Zechariah 3:4). You can trust Him for this. There is no greater love in this world than the love of the Son of God. It is for want of this love that the world is perishing.

Specifically, we need "faith in His blood" (Romans 3:25, KJV). In the upper room Jesus said, "This is My blood of the new covenant, which is shed for many for the remission of sins" (Matthew 26:28). "Sin is lawlessness" (1 John 3:4), and Jesus said plainly that His blood is able to "remit" or remove our sins. John cried, "To Him who loved us and washed us from our sins in His own blood" (Revelation 1:5).

Can we believe what we can't fully explain? Of course. I can't explain how my heart beats, but I'm positive that it does. I can't explain how my brain works, but I'm thankful for every intricate chemical and electrical function. Similarly, I can't explain exactly how the blood of Jesus Christ has the power to cleanse an entire lost world from its sins of breaking the Ten Commandments. But I know it is true. It is so, because the Bible says so.

The true message of the third angel places tremendous emphasis on the blood of Jesus Christ.

The Lord in His great mercy sent a most precious message to His people through Elders Waggoner and Jones. . . . The efficacy of the blood of Christ was to be presented to the people with freshness and power, that their faith might lay hold of its merits. . . . Every sin acknowledged before God with a contrite heart He will remove. This faith is the life of the church.[21]

Satan desires the death of the church. He is a god of death (see Hebrews 2:14). Just look at online music sellers and see the covers of so many CDs sporting skulls, crossbones, cemeteries, and coffins. I know. I used to listen to some of those very songs. It's ghastly. Satan knows the life of the church depends upon faith in the blood of Jesus. That's why he wants this subject dead and buried.

It's time for a resurrection.

"The true religion, the only religion of the Bible" is "believing in the forgiveness of sins, the righteousness of Christ, and the blood of the Lamb."[22] This is true religion. All else is a counterfeit. "Faith seizes and appropriates the righteousness of Christ. . . . Let the sinner by faith appropriate the merits of the blood of a crucified Redeemer to his own case—'the Lord my righteousness.' "[23] Yes, Jesus is OUR RIGHTEOUSNESS. We must trust Him for this. His blood was shed FOR YOU. You must believe it. Your personal faith must "appropriate the merits of the blood of a crucified Redeemer" to your "own case" and apply the cleansing blood of Christ to cover your personal sins of breaking the Ten Commandments. If you do, here is God's promise: " 'Though your sins are like scarlet, they shall be as white as snow' " (Isaiah 1:18). Believe it.

On the night Israel left Egypt, God Almighty told His people, " 'Take some of the blood and put it on the two doorposts and on the lintel of the houses' " (Exodus 12:7). The Lord declared, " 'When I see the blood, I will pass over you' " (Exodus 12:13). This was the birthday of the Israelite nation. It was born by blood. Less than a year after the Minneapolis conference, Ellen White wrote, "Strike the doorposts with the blood of Calvary's Lamb, and you are safe."[24] The "strike" of faith in the blood of Jesus will give our souls a birthday into a new life. God Himself will "pass over" our sins and we will be "justified by His blood" (Romans 5:9). Alleluia! It is a living truth that "the blood of Jesus Christ His Son cleanses us from all sin" (1 John 1:7).

In a chapter on the Passover, Ellen White wrote,

> The merits of Christ's blood must be applied to the soul. We must believe, not only that He died for the world, but that He died for us individually. We must appropriate to ourselves the virtue of the atoning sacrifice.[25]

The only safety for the Israelites was blood upon the doorposts. God said, "When I see the blood, I will pass over you" (Exodus 12:13). All other devices for safety would be without avail. Nothing but the blood on the doorposts would bar the way that the angel of death should not enter.

> There is salvation for the sinner in the blood of Jesus Christ alone, which cleanseth us from all sin. The man with a cultivated intellect may have vast stores of knowledge, he may engage in theological speculations, he may be great and honored of men and be considered the repository of knowledge, but unless he has a saving knowledge of Christ crucified for him, and by faith lays hold upon the righteousness of Christ, he is lost.[26]

I am Jewish myself (at least three-fourths). I am also the firstborn of my mother. Believe me, if I were in Egypt when the angel of death passed through, I would have taken great pains to make sure that my dad put that blood on our door. Yet, in Egypt it was only a person's earthly life at stake. Now our souls hang in the balance. We cannot afford to make any mistakes in this matter. We have been told that if we do not "by faith lay hold" upon "the merits of Christ's blood," we are lost. Eternally lost. The popular phrase, "You only go around once in life," will come truth for those who fail to trust in the blood of Jesus. Commenting upon Romans 3:23, 24, E. J. Waggoner wrote,

> All have sinned, and all are guilty before God, and the only way that any can escape final condemnation is by faith in the blood of Christ. All who believe on Him are justified freely by the grace of God, and His righteousness is imputed to them although they have violated the law.[27]

In her article, "Experience Following the 1888 Minneapolis Conference; The Danger of Legalism; Emphasizing Religious Liberty," Ellen White urged Adventist ministers to "talk it. Pray it. Without the shedding of blood there is no remission of sins. Then why not dwell upon the necessity of faith in the blood of Jesus Christ?"[28]

"How much more shall the blood of Christ, who through the eternal Spirit offered himself without spot to God, purge your conscience from dead works to serve the living God?" (Hebrews 9:14).

Perhaps the most famous allegory ever penned is John Bunyan's *Pilgrim's Progress,* illustrating the perils and possibilities of the Christian life. In the story, Mr. Christian journeyed toward the Celestial City with a terrible burden on his back. After climbing a hill, he reached the cross. There—to his great joy—his heavy burden rolled off his back and down the hill. This will happen to us when we have simple faith, like a little child, in the blood of Jesus Christ. His blood will purge our consciences from the crushing weight of being "guilty before God" (Romans 3:19). The awful sense of the condemnation of the law will roll away.

I can't explain it. But I know it is true.

It happened to me.

Jesus alone can deliver us from bondage to "dead works" (Hebrews 9:14). What are "dead works"? They are our own works of endlessly striving to make ourselves acceptable to God. They are "dead works" because they lead to a Dead End. We cannot earn, or work for, or merit the forgiveness of Jesus. But when we bring to God the merits of Christ, trusting alone in His shed blood, we will be "justified freely by His grace through the redemption that is in Christ Jesus" (Romans 3:24). Freedom from guilt does not come through our attainments but through faith in His atonement. With our guilt removed we can finally "serve the living God." This is real *Pilgrim's Progress.* Praise the Lord!

Many people are now wasting away inside insane asylums because of guilt. One of the biggest failures of modern psychology stems from the fact that it so often misses the boat in understanding that guilt in the human conscience is often rooted in breaking the Ten Commandments. Few trained therapists know "this truth" about the law, sin, guilt, and the solution of the blood of Jesus. Some well-known psychologists have made fortunes counseling people whose underlying problems stem from guilt because of sin. Guilt can cause stress, sickness, and can easily destroy the joy of living.

A guilt-ridden man once visited his doctor. He felt pain in his back, chest, and head. After running a series of tests, the doctor declared, "I can't seem to find any physical causes for your condition."

"What do I do?" the burdened man replied.

After thinking for a moment, the doctor replied, "I've got it! You need something to cheer you up. Go downtown to Fifth and Main tomorrow night. There is a clown there who performs for the kids at the school. He's really funny. Maybe laughter will soothe your mind and relieve your symptoms."

The patient removed his glasses. With dark eyes of desperation he then looked at the doctor. "Doc," he moaned woefully, "I am that clown!"

Dear reader, the solution to humanity's universal problem of guilt is not laughter, rationalization, drugs, alcohol, sex, entertainment, self-help books, expensive therapy, or even good works. Not at all. Instead, we need a biblical solution. According to God's Book, guilt can be permanently removed from the conscience only by faith in the blood of the Lord Jesus Christ.

But there is another vital point that must not be left out. Scripture also in-separably combines "repentance toward God" with "faith toward our Lord Jesus Christ" (Acts 20:21). Jesus urged, "Repent, and believe in the gospel" (Mark

1:15). Solomon wrote, "He who covers his sins will not prosper, but whoever confesses and forsakes them will have mercy" (Proverbs 28:13). True faith and repentance are like two sides of the same coin. In other words, real faith takes hold of the promises of God with both hands, and one of those hands cannot cling to sin at the same time. Notice carefully: We do not have to become righteous first in order for God to remove our guilt, for this is impossible. But still, we must make a choice to let go of every known sin. This is not a good work to earn His favor but simply fulfilling His reasonable condition. Because God is just, He can "be just" and "the justifier" (Romans 3:26) of only those who repent and have "faith in Jesus."

Ezekiel wrote, "Repent, and turn from all your transgressions, so that iniquity will not be your ruin" (Ezekiel 18:30). Ellen White agreed: "Everything that is offensive to God must be put away."[29] "God requires the entire surrender of the heart before justification can take place."[30] "A sinner is justified before God when he repents of his sins."[31] "God receives, pardons, justifies, the repentant, believing soul."[32] "The righteousness of Christ will not cover one cherished sin."[33] "Christ must be lifted up, because He is a Savior who forgiveth transgression, iniquity and sin, but will by no means clear the guilty and unrepentant soul."[34] While some may not like it, we must accept the simple Bible truth that "sins that are not confessed will never be forgiven."[35]

Why should we hesitate to surrender every sin to Jesus? If we struggle here, we should ponder these penetrating questions:

> Do you feel that it is too great a sacrifice to yield all to Christ? Ask yourself the question, "What has Christ given for me?" The Son of God gave all—life and love and suffering—for our redemption. And can it be that we, the unworthy objects of so great love, will withhold our hearts from Him?[36]

Can it be? As we behold Christ's love as He hung dying upon the cross, how can we not make a full surrender? As we behold Jesus being separated from His Father in Gethsemane and on Calvary, how can we stubbornly refuse to be separated from our sins?

The revelation of such love should make it easy to cut loose of every wicked thing. Think soberly. What has sin ever done for us anyway? Like the Black Death that devastated Europe in the 1300s, it will only obliterate us. Why not look sin square in the face and say "Goodbye" forever? Someone once correctly stated, "If Jesus is not Lord of all, then He is not Lord at all." We can't ride the fence. Being 99 percent for Jesus while even 1 percent for sin actually places us 100 percent on Satan's turf. The Bible testifies:

"Nevertheless the solid foundation of God stands, having this seal: 'The Lord knows those who are His,' and, 'Let everyone who names the name of Christ depart from iniquity' "(2 Timothy 2:19).

Our loving Savior left a holy heaven and came down to this dark world. Here, He "lived a sinless life. He died for us. Now He offers to take our sins and give us His righteousness."[37] This is His trillion-dollar offer. Will you accept it? Will the righteousness of Christ be transferred to your account or not? The next sentence specifies both the condition and the promise.

If you give yourself to Him, and accept Him as your Savior, then, sinful as your life may have been, for His sake you are accounted righteous. Christ's character stands in the place of your character, and you are accepted before God just as if you had not sinned.[38]

At the 1893 General Conference Session, A. T. Jones spoke to the delegates:

He gave Himself for our sins. Then I say again, and you see, that it is simply with you and me a living choice, as to whether we will have the Lord or ourselves, the Lord's righteousness or our sins, the Lord's way or our way? Which will we have? [Congregation: "The Lord's way."[39]

Good choice!

Jones's words remind me of a story about a young boy determined to outwit an old Chinese sage. With a living bird hidden trapped in his hands, the youth asked the wise elder, "Is the bird in my hands alive or dead?"

If the old man responded, "Alive," the boy would crush it quickly and prove the sage wrong. But if he answered, "Dead," he would triumphantly open his hands and let the bird fly away.

As is often the case, age was smarter than youth. The old sage responded, "As you choose, so shall it be."

The same is true with salvation. If we choose to surrender all to Jesus, the books of record, though hidden, will bear witness to the fact on Judgment Day. The righteousness of Christ will be transferred to our account and we will be accepted before God. Yet if we choose to hold on to our sins, our guilty record will remain. The living choice is ours. "As you choose," so shall it be. Someday, we will end up either "dead or alive." In 1888, "At Minneapolis . . . they would have had a rich experience. But self said, No. . . . Self struggled for the mastery."[40] Here is the real battlefield. It's like the Gaza Strip—a Middle East area so often torn by war—of our souls.

Again, the issue is not works but surrender.

Will we fully surrender self or not?

A rebellious young man in his twenties lived for no one but himself. After committing some crimes, he was finally arrested and thrown in jail. After serving his sentence, he went to look for his old buddies. Having nowhere to stay his first night of being free, he remembered his mother and decided to pop over. The last time he had seen her was at the courthouse, at his trial. There, she was plump and rosy but tearful.

He knocked once. Then twice. When the door was finally opened by a worn, gray-haired old woman, he didn't realize at first what had happened. For a second or two, he just stared. When the truth finally hit him that this was his mom, he cried, "Oh, Mother, what have I done to you?" Then came those tears of repentance that neither punishment nor prison had ever wrung from him.

Peter said, "God has made this Jesus, whom you crucified, both Lord and Christ" (Acts 2:36). When we finally grasp that our sins of breaking God's law have crucified Jesus Christ Himself, this will motivate us to make a full surrender as nothing else can. We will cry out, "Oh, Jesus, what have I done to you?" Not wanting to hurt Jesus anymore, we will renounce sin with loathing. "Wicked sins, I hate you," will be the cry of our hearts. As we fully "behold what manner of love the Father has bestowed on us" (1 John 3:1), this will lift our motive to surrender high above mere fear of punishment or hope of reward.

> The theme that attracts the heart of the sinner is Christ, and Him crucified. On the cross of Calvary, Jesus stands revealed to the world in unparalleled love. Present Him thus to the hungering multitudes, and the light of His love will win men from darkness to light, from transgression to obedience and true holiness.
>
> Beholding Jesus upon the cross of Calvary arouses the conscience to the heinous character of sin as nothing else can do. It was sin that caused the death of God's dear Son, and sin is the transgression of the law. On Him was laid the iniquities of us all. The sinner then consents unto the law that it is good; for he realizes that it condemns his evil deeds, while he magnifies the matchless love of God in providing for him salvation through the imputed righteousness of Him who knew no sin, in whose mouth there was found no guile.[41]

> Justification by faith is to many a mystery. A sinner is justified by God when he repents of his sins. He sees Jesus upon the cross of Calvary. Why all this suffering? The law of Jehovah has been broken . . . and the penalty of sin is pronounced to be death. But, "God so loved the world, that He gave His only begotten Son, that whosoever believeth on

Him should not perish, but have everlasting life." Oh, what love, what matchless love! Christ, the Son of God, dying for guilty man. The sinner views the spirituality of the law of God and its eternal obligations. He sees the love of God in providing a substitute and surety for guilty man, and that Substitute is One Equal with God.

This display of grace in the gift of salvation to the world fills the sinner with amazement. This love of God to man breaks every barrier down. He comes to the cross, which has been placed midway between divinity and humanity, and repents of his sins of transgression, because Christ has been drawing him to Himself. He does not expect the law to cleanse him from sin, for there is no pardoning quality in the law to save the transgressor of the law. He looks to the atoning sacrifice as his only hope, through repentance toward God—because the laws of His government have been broken—and faith toward our Lord Jesus Christ as the One who can save and cleanse the sinner from every transgression. . . . Sinners can be justified by God only when He pardons their sins, remits the punishment they deserve, and treats them as though they were really just, receiving them into divine favor and treating them as if they were righteous. They are justified alone through the imputed righteousness of Christ.[42]

This is the heart of *God's Last Message: Christ Our Righteousness,* and the living center of the third angel's message. Ellen White referred to it as "the matchless charms of Christ."[43] In these "last days" (2 Timothy 3:1) of mesmerizing Hollywood entertainment, the eyes of mankind must somehow be torn away from soap operas, hi-tech glitter, fanciful glamour, and even from their own puny efforts to obey God, to behold Jesus hanging upon the tree. At Minneapolis, "The Lord in His great mercy sent a most precious message to His people through Elders Waggoner and Jones. . . . Many had lost sight of Jesus. They needed to have their eyes directed to His divine person, His merits, and His changeless love for the human family."[44]

Today, even many church members have "lost sight of Jesus" and grope in darkness. Unsatisfied, many longingly inquire as in days of old, "Sir, we wish to see Jesus" (John 12:21).

Shall we not reveal Him?

If not now, when? If not you, who?

Jesus said, "No one can come to Me unless the Father who sent Me draws him" (John 6:44). "And I, if I am lifted up from the earth, will draw all peoples to Myself" (John 12:32). Jesus is seeking to draw every human being on planet

Earth to Himself. Humanity is so utterly helpless that we can't even get started on our own. Just as a car can't go anywhere until the driver first turns on the ignition key, so it is with us in this life. Even the ability to repent, confess our sins, and have faith in Christ's blood is a gift of His grace. Jesus is our "Prince and . . . Savior, to give repentance to Israel and forgiveness of sins" (Acts 5:31). Ellen White commented, "We can no more repent without the Spirit of Christ to awaken the conscience than we can be pardoned without Christ."[45] Jesus must first wake up our world-deadened consciences before we will even want to arise out of sin's bed.

It's time to wake up. Those who remain wrapped in sin's slumber are ruining themselves. Satan has an endless supply of sleeping pills. But Heaven's alarm clock is sounding, " 'Awake, you who sleep, arise from the dead, and Christ will give you light' " (Ephesians 5:14). Oh that "God . . . will grant them repentance, so that they may know the truth . . . that they may come to their senses and escape the snare of the devil, having been taken captive by him to do his will" (2 Timothy 2:25, 26).

Many so-called "recovery" programs exist today to pacify and heal human ills. But the most important one is the Righteousness by Faith Recovery From the Devil program centered in the grace of Jesus Christ.

May His love capture our hearts!

Paul wrote, "The goodness of God leads you to repentance" (Romans 2:4). Ellen White commented,

> Christ must be revealed to the sinner as the Savior dying for the sins of the world; and as we behold the Lamb of God upon the cross of Calvary, the mystery of redemption begins to unfold to our minds and the goodness of God leads us to repentance. In dying for sinners, Christ manifested a love that is incomprehensible; and as the sinner beholds this love, it softens the heart, impresses the mind, and inspires contrition in the soul. . . . The sinner may resist this love, may refuse to be drawn to Christ; but if he does not resist he will be drawn to Jesus; a knowledge of the plan of salvation will lead him to the foot of the cross in repentance for his sins, which have caused the suffering of God's dear Son.[46]

The love of Jesus is a magnet constantly drawing our hearts to Him. Why resist Him? Why put on the breaks? If you do, you're only wounding your own soul, risking eternity, and edging one step closer to "the lake of fire," which is "the second death" (Revelation 20:14).

In these traumatic days of devastating earthquakes, tsunamis, fires, hurricanes, drought, doubt, devilish doctrines, and global confusion, *God's Last Message:*

Christ Our Righteousness proclaims "justification through faith in the Surety."[47] Jesus alone is our Surety. His word is "the prophetic word confirmed" (2 Peter 1:19). Christ is "an anchor of the soul, both sure and steadfast" (Hebrews 6:19).

> By His perfect obedience He has satisfied the claims of the law, and my hope is found in looking to Him as my substitute and surety, who obeyed the law perfectly for me. By faith in His merits I am free from the condemnation of the law. He clothes me with His righteousness, which answers all the demands of the law. I am complete in Him who brings in everlasting righteousness. He presents me to God in the spotless garment of which no thread was woven by any human agent. All is of Christ, and all the glory, honor, and majesty are to be given to the Lamb of God, which taketh away the sins of the world.[48]

Gabriel predicted that the Messiah would "bring in everlasting righteousness" (Daniel 9:24). He has, and it is available to us right now by faith.

> The provision made is complete, and the eternal righteousness of Christ is placed to the account of every believing soul. The costly, spotless robe, woven in the loom of heaven, has been provided for the repenting, believing sinner, and he may say: "I will greatly rejoice in the Lord, my soul shall be joyful in my God; for He hath clothed me with the garments of salvation, He hath covered me with the robe of righteousness" (Isaiah 61:10).[49]

For us, this royal robe is a free gift.

For Jesus, it cost Him His life.

God's Last Message: Christ Our Righteousness, which is the third angel's message, proclaims "the commandments of God" and "the faith of Jesus" (Revelation 14:12). But what exactly is the "faith of Jesus"? Speculation exists in some Adventist circles, but here is an inspired answer.

> The third angel's message is the proclamation of the commandments of God and the faith of Jesus Christ. . . . "The faith of Jesus." It is talked of, but not understood. What constitutes the faith of Jesus, that belongs to the third angel's message? Jesus becoming our Sin-Bearer that He might become our sin pardoning Savior. He was treated as we deserve to be treated. He came to our world and took our sins that we might take His righteousness. Faith in the ability of Christ to save us amply and fully and entirely is the faith of Jesus.[50]

There it is. Jesus Christ can do it. After His death, burial, and resurrection, Jesus ascended triumphantly to heaven, and He can get us there too!

"He who believes in Me," our Lord promises, "has everlasting life" (John 6:47). Again, "He who believes in Him is not condemned" (John 3:18). In "Looking Back at Minneapolis," Ellen White enthusiastically wrote that "the most precious light . . . of the great subject of the righteousness of Christ connected with the law" should "constantly be kept before the sinner as his only hope of salvation."[51] How often is "constantly"? "The sinner must ever look to Calvary; and with the simple faith of a little child, he must rest in the merits of Christ, accepting His righteousness and believing in His mercy."[52]

Does our heavenly Father love us? Yes. So why not "rest in the merits of Christ" and enjoy a "full and complete pardon for sin" through the blood of Jesus?

The last book in the Bible reports,

> "To Him who loved us and washed us from our sins in His own blood, and has made us kings and priests to His God and Father, to Him be glory and dominion forever and ever. Amen" (Revelation 1:5, 6).

Alleluia!

I get excited about this message. I'm sure my Lord is not bothered in the least.

---

1. *1888 Materials,* 1055.
2. Ibid., 211.
3. *Signs of the Times,* Sept. 2, 1886.
4. White, *Steps to Christ,* 51.
5. White, *Mount of Blessing,* 116.
6. White, *Steps to Christ,* 62.
7. *Signs of the Times,* November 30, 1891.
8. White, *Our High Calling,* 53.
9. White, *Selected Messages,* 1:392.
10. *1888 Materials,* 164.
11. *1888 Materials,* 518.
12. *The Review and Herald,* November 22, 1892.
13. White, *Gospel Workers,* 161.
14. White, *Patriarchs and Prophets,* 309.
15. White, *Selected Messages,* 1:235.
16. Ibid., 377.

17. White, *Steps to Christ,* 37.

18. *The Review and Herald,* November 4, 1890.

19. White, *Selected Messages,* 1:389.

20. White, *Steps to Christ,* 52, 53.

21. White, *Testimonies to Ministers,* 91–93.

22. *1888 Materials,* 948.

23. Ibid., 373, 375.

24. *The Review and Herald,* September 3, 1889.

25. White, *Patriarchs and Prophets,* 277.

26. *1888 Materials,* 218.

27. E. J. Waggoner, *The Gospel in the Book of Galatians* (Oakland, CA: publisher unknown, 1888), 5.

28. *1888 Materials,* 372.

29. White, *Steps to Christ,* 39.

30. White, *Selected Messages,* 1:366.

31. White, *Selected Messages,* 3:194.

32. White, *Selected Messages,* 1:367.

33. White, *Christ's Object Lessons,* 316.

34. *The Review and Herald,* August 13, 1889.

35. *The Review and Herald,* December 16, 1890.

36. White, *Steps to Christ,* 45.

37. Ibid., 62.

38. Ibid.

39. *1893 General Conference Bulletin,* 404.

40. *1888 Materials,* 1030.

41. *The Review and Herald,* November 22, 1892.

42. White, *Selected Messages,* 3:194, 195.

43. Manuscript 5, 1889.

44. White, *Testimonies to Ministers,* 91, 92.

45. White, *Steps to Christ,* 26.

46. Ibid., 26, 27.

47. White, *Testimonies to Ministers,* 91.

48. White, *Selected Messages,* 1:396.

49. Ibid., 394.

50. *1888 Materials,* 217.

51. Ibid., 212.

52. *The Review and Herald,* March 20, 1894.

CHAPTER FOURTEEN

HIS PRESENCE ON THE INSIDE

"WHAT COMES FROM THE HEART, GOES TO THE HEART."
—German proverb

B lessed are those who hunger and thirst for righteousness, for they shall be
filled" (Matthew 5:6). "As many as received Him, to them He gave the
right to become children of God, to those who believe in His name" (John
1:12). "That Christ may dwell in your hearts through faith" (Ephesians 3:17).
"[God] purifying their hearts by faith" (Acts 15:9).

If your kitchen drain is throwing up sludge, you need to do more than wipe
up the mess. The problem must be solved underneath the sink. Likewise, we
need more than the imputed righteousness of Christ to cover our sinful past.
We also need His Presence on the Inside to prevent the continual flowing of
more garbage into the world.

The Bible clearly reveals the dual nature of humanity's sin problem: (1) a
sinful past and (2) a selfish heart. We cannot solve either problem ourselves,
but Jesus can. "You cannot atone for your past sins [Problem 1]; you cannot
change your heart and make yourself holy [Problem 2]. But God promises to
do all this for you through Christ."[1] The eighth essential element of *God's Last
Message: Christ Our Righteousness,* which the Lord "sent to His people through
Elders Waggoner and Jones" in 1888, is that Jesus is now "imparting the priceless gift of His own righteousness to the helpless human agent."[2]

The third angel's message provides the solution to the deepest problems
facing the entire human family. Every person around the world needs (1) freedom from guilt and (2) supernatural power to transform the heart. This is
exactly what Jesus Christ now offers. Notice carefully, "God's forgiveness is not
merely a judicial act by which He sets us free from condemnation. It is not only

forgiveness for sin, but reclaiming from sin. It is the outflow of redeeming love that transforms the heart."[3] Thus biblical justification, which is the forgiveness of sins, is (1) a judicial act that frees us from the condemnation of the law and (2) the channel for God's redeeming love to transform our hearts and rescue us from sin.

To put it simply, those whom God forgives, *He changes.*

Paul wrote about "the righteousness of God apart from the law . . . revealed . . . through faith in Jesus Christ, to all and on all who believe" (Romans 3:21, 22). The Greek word for "to" in this sentence literally means "into." E. J. Waggoner commented in *Signs,*

> Note also that the righteousness by faith of Jesus Christ is "unto all and upon all them that believe." On the word rendered "unto," Prof. James R. Boise has this excellent note: "Not simply unto, in the sense of to, towards, up to, as the word is commonly understood; but into (in the strict and usual sense of *eis* [the Greek word for unto]), entering into the heart, into the inner being of all those who have faith." This is exactly in accordance with God's promise in the covenant: "I will put My law in their inward parts, and write it in their hearts" (Jeremiah 31:33). The righteousness that comes by faith is not superficial; it is actual; and is made a part of the individual.[4]

This "priceless gift" of the righteousness of Jesus Christ, which is "made a part of the individual," is ministered by the Lord "to the helpless human agent."[5] Like a child lost in the snow, we are helpless. Mr. Christian in *Pilgrim's Progress* could not remove the terrible burden clinging to his back. "It is impossible for us, of ourselves, to escape from the pit of sin in which we are sunken. Our hearts are evil, and we cannot change them."[6] "Since we are sinful, unholy, we cannot perfectly obey the holy law."[7] Ah, but we can come to Jesus in our helplessness. "Jesus loves to have us come just as we are, sinful, helpless, dependent."[8]

At the 1893 General Conference Session, Elder A. T. Jones, after reading the above sentence from *Steps to Christ* to the delegates, commented, "What is 'sinful?' [Congregation: 'Full of sin.'] Does Jesus love to have us come to Him just as we are, full of sin? [Congregation: 'Yes.'] Does He? [Congregation: 'Yes, sir.']."[9]

Do you believe that?

Ellen White continued:

> We may come with all our weakness, our folly, our sinfulness, and fall at His feet in penitence. It is His glory to encircle us in the arms of

His love and to bind up our wounds, to cleanse us from all impurity. . . . None are so sinful that they cannot find strength, purity, and righteousness in Jesus, who died for them.[10]

Christ connects fallen man in His weakness and helplessness with the Source of infinite power.[11]

The righteousness of God is embodied in Christ. We receive righteousness by receiving Him. . . . Not by painful struggles or wearisome toil, not by gift or sacrifice, is righteousness obtained; but it is given freely to every soul who hungers and thirst to receive it. . . . "This is His Name whereby He shall be called, The Lord Our Righteousness."[12]

This "most precious message" that dawned upon Adventists in Minneapolis, Minnesota, in the year 1888, "invited the people to receive the righteousness of Christ, which is made manifest in obedience to all the commandments of God."[13] Notice carefully that it is "the righteousness of Christ" which is to be "made manifest." We cannot be justified or saved by our own works, nor can we change our hearts and keep God's law in our own strength. Yet at the same time, "man can never be saved in disobedience."[14] If we are only willing to give up sin and submit to Jesus, His power upon us and within us will be "manifest" through a life of obedience. "That your faith should not be in the wisdom of men but in the power of God" (1 Corinthians 2:5). Paul rejoiced that in his "weakness . . . the power of Christ may rest upon me" (2 Corinthians 12:9).

In 1893, Ellen White explained more fully,

While we cannot do anything to change our hearts or to bring ourselves into harmony with God; while we must not trust at all [how much?] to ourselves or to our good works, our lives will reveal whether the grace of God is dwelling within us.[15]

Elder Jones commented on this exact sentence at the 1893 General Conference Session: "You see then, God's idea is that when He is there, He will show Himself through us."[16]

This is what we need.

We need Jesus to "show Himself through us."

In the beginning, God made Adam and Eve "in His own image" (Genesis 1:27) to reflect His glory. But when the sly serpent tricked Eve, both she and her husband plunged into sin. But through the plan of salvation, God's original desire "that the life of Jesus also may be manifested in our mortal flesh"

(2 Corinthians 4:11) can once again begin to be realized. Ultimately, Heaven's goal is "Christ in you, the hope of glory" (Colossians 1:27). Jesus said, "I delight to do Your will, O my God, and Your law is within my heart" (Psalm 40:8; see Hebrews 10:7). When Christ comes into human hearts, He brings His righteousness with Him, and the result is a life of obedience to the law of God. "Instead of releasing man from obedience, it is faith, and faith alone, that makes us partakers of the grace of Christ, which enables us to render obedience."[17] Waggoner wrote that when a man "has Christ, he must have the law; for Christ is the embodiment of the law."[18] Again, "Righteousness—conformity to the law—comes alone through faith in Christ."[19]

Our Savior tells His true followers, "If you love Me, keep My commandments" (John 14:15). Notice carefully the connection between love and law. The only way to "keep" is through "love." And the only way to "love" is to first realize His infinite love for us! As it is written, "We love Him because He first loved us" (1 John 4:19). "If our hearts are renewed in the likeness of God, if the divine love is implanted in the soul, will not the law be carried out in the life?"[20] It will. Thus if we want more obedience to the law, we must receive more of the love of Jesus Christ.

Just to clarify. Obedience doesn't earn us anything. Think about it. If a mother tells her son to take out the trash, and he obeys, does this earn her love? Of course not. In the same way, "We do not earn salvation by our obedience, for salvation is the free gift of God, to be received by faith. But obedience is the fruit of faith."[21] But what if the boy rebelliously refused to take out the garbage? What would that say about his love for his mother? It's the same with us and our Savior. Obedience is the test of our love. "Here is the true test. If we abide in Christ, if the love of God dwells in us, our feelings, our thoughts, our purposes, our actions, will be in harmony with the will of God as expressed in the precepts of His holy law."[22]

I spent many years in school taking quizzes, midterms, tests, and final exams. According to the Bible, God also has one basic test for us. Ellen White called it "the true test." It is a test of obedience, and love is the only way to pass. As it is written, "Love is the fulfillment of the law" (Romans 13:10). "Obedience—the service and allegiance of love—is the true sign of discipleship."[23] Those who pass this test will receive Eternal Diplomas on Graduation Day, for it is written again, "Blessed are those who do His commandments, that they may have the right to the tree of life, and may enter through the gates into the city" (Revelation 22:14).

This is God's Word, not my opinion.

If you asked a decent-hearted father why he would never kill his own kids, would he say, "Because there is a law in my state against killing children. I would go to jail"? Or would he say, "Because the sixth commandment says, 'Thou shalt not kill' "? Of course not. The reason a good dad would never do such a horrible thing is that he loves his little ones. This is the same reason the Bible gives for us to keep His commandments. As it is written, "This is the love of God, that we keep His commandments" (1 John 5:3).

Without love, there is no real keeping of the law. Just formalism.

According to the book of Romans, the heavenly message of "having been justified by faith" (Romans 5:1) is actually the purest channel for "the love of God" to be "poured out in our hearts by the Holy Spirit who was given to us" (Romans 5:5). Notice carefully. The coming of the Holy Spirit is revealed as a gift. Peter said, "Repent, and let every one of you be baptized in the name of Jesus Christ for the remission of sins; and you shall receive the gift of the Holy Spirit" (Acts 2:38). Don't miss this sequence. Paul and Peter agreed that (1) we must first be "justified" for the "remission of sins"; (2) then we can "receive the gift of the Holy Spirit"; (3) then, and only then, with "the love of God" in our hearts, can we obey the Master's call, "If you love Me, keep My commandments" (John 14:15). If we forget this order, our lives will be filled with these three *D*s: Disorder, Discouragement, and Despair, which come from the devil.

Don't be duped!

According to Paul, it is through the biblical message of "having been justified by faith" (Romans 5:1) that our Lord Jesus Christ "imparts the priceless gift of His own righteousness to the helpless human agent."[24] It is through the gift of "the special power of the Holy Spirit" that we helpless sinners can be "enabled to keep the law." It is through *God's Last Message: Christ Our Righteousness* that "the righteous requirement of the law might be fulfilled in us who do not walk according to the flesh but according to the Spirit" (Romans 8:4). And it is through the third angel's message of "the righteousness of Christ in connection with the law" which E. J. Waggoner preached at Minneapolis in 1888 that this group of apocalyptic "saints" will finally be produced: "Here is the patience of the saints; here are those who keep the commandments of God and the faith of Jesus" (Revelation 14:12).

Again, keep in mind that the performance of good works has absolutely no place in biblical justification. "A man is justified by faith apart from the deeds of the law" (Romans 3:28), penned the apostle. "God imputes righteousness apart from works" (Romans 4:6). Yet, when Christ enters the heart through faith, we are "created in Christ Jesus for good works, which God prepared beforehand that we should walk in them" (Ephesians 2:10). Those who are "justified by His grace" will "be careful to maintain good works" (Titus 3:7, 8). "But Christ, after having redeemed man from the condemnation of the law [justification], could impart divine power to unite with human effort."[25] Then with this "special power of the Holy Spirit" united with our human efforts, we can finally make real *Pilgrim's Progress* in our journey to the Celestial City.

True "faith [works] through love" (Galatians 5:6). This is the only thing that really works! Everything else doesn't work and needs fixing. Trying to work in order to be justified or accepted by God brings nothing but dreary bondage and a dead end. It's like trying to drive a car before putting gas in the tank. Have you ever seen a hamster jogging around and around in a wheel inside its cage? It gets nowhere. Neither will we unless we focus on God's grace. Babylon has "fallen" and has become "a cage for every unclean and hated bird!" (Revelation 18:2). The third angel's message reveals that the only hope for anyone who has "sinned and fall[en] short of the glory of God" is "being justified freely by His grace through the redemption that is in Christ Jesus" (Romans 3:23, 24).

In his fiery letter to the Galatians, Paul rebuked his own converts who had been led astray from "this truth." With deep passion he inquired,

> O foolish Galatians! Who has bewitched you that you should not obey the truth, before whose eyes Jesus Christ was clearly portrayed among you as crucified? This only I want to learn from you: Did you receive the Spirit by the works of the law, or by the hearing of faith? (Galatians 3:1, 2).

These Galatian converts had earlier received the Spirit, not through a focus on their own puny "works of the law," but rather through faith in the Crucified One. But through satanic subtlety they had been bewitched into turning their eyes away from Calvary. As a result, like a mass of rotting flesh, their spiritual life was fast decomposing. But faith in Jesus would revive them. This would reopen the door for the Holy Spirit to enter. Then, once again, their good works by God's power would advance the truth. Shortly after the Minneapolis General Conference, Ellen White wrote, "The present message, justification by faith—is a message from God; it bears the divine credentials, for its fruit is unto holiness."[26] This message is the channel for Heaven's power. It is the door through which we can receive the imparted righteousness of Jesus Christ. The God who caused lightning to flash and thunder to roll on Mount Sinai will freely impart the infinite power of His Holy Spirit to us when we have faith in Him who died for us on Calvary. The God who wrote with His finger the Ten Commandments on a rock speaks of those who trust in the blood of Jesus. "I will put My laws into their mind, and write them in their hearts" (Hebrews 8:10). This "new" covenant is based on the "better promises" of Jesus Christ. Read Hebrews 8:6, 8–10. Jesus does for us what we can't do for ourselves.

This results in a new experience.

The Holy Spirit, who enters our hearts through the channel of justification by faith, is mightier than human flesh.

Sin could be resisted and overcome only through the mighty agency of the Third Person of the Godhead, who would come with no modified energy, but in the fullness of divine power. . . . Christ has given His Spirit as a divine power to overcome all hereditary and cultivated tendencies to evil, and to impress His own character upon His church.[27]

Jesus Christ "has made provision that the Holy Spirit shall be imparted to every repentant soul, to keep him from sinning."[28] Instead of working to earn His favor, we should "submit . . . therefore to God," and in His power "resist the devil and he will flee from you" (James 4:7). When Satan knocks at your heart's door, send Jesus to open it. Quote Scripture!

Today's news headlines proclaim in thunderous tones louder than on Mount Sinai "the corruption that is in the world through lust" (2 Peter 1:4). Daily reports in newspapers, on the radio, and on CNN make the heart sick. Our world is enslaved by sin. Jesus said, "Whoever commits sin is a slave of sin" (John 8:34). He alone has power to deliver. "If the Son makes you free, you shall be free indeed" (John 8:36). When properly understood, *God's Last Message: Christ Our Righteousness* reveals that "all power is given into His hands, that He may dispense rich gifts unto men, imparting the priceless gift of His own righteousness to the helpless human agent."[29] More than one hundred years ago E. J. Waggoner wrote in *Signs,* "Christ comes into the heart, not because it is free from sin, but in order to free it from sin."[30] His ancient article is living truth for us today. Waggoner's works still follow him (see Revelation 14:13).

A genuine Christian should be different from the average sinner. A famous story is told of a young soldier who fought in the army of Alexander the Great. In a certain battle the youth turned coward and fled. Later he was brought before Alexander.

"Soldier, what's your name?" the general inquired.

"Alexander," replied the young man. After reflecting a moment, the Macedonian prince said boldly, "Soldier, either change your conduct, or change your name."

It's the same for us. Again, Paul wrote, " 'Let everyone who names the name of Christ depart from iniquity' " (2 Timothy 2:19).

To "depart" means to leave.

We should leave sin immediately.

Jesus Christ has infinite power to "save His people from their sins" (Matthew 1:21). Jesus said, "A disciple is not above his teacher, but everyone who is perfectly trained will be like his teacher" (Luke 6:40). We are to become like Him by His grace. Peter revealed the purpose of grace. "May the God of all grace, who called us to His eternal glory by Christ Jesus, after you have suffered a while, perfect, establish, strengthen, and settle you. To Him be the glory and the dominion forever and ever" (1 Peter 5:10, 11). When we are justified by His grace and no longer guilty before God, we need not fear a high standard. The goal of Christianity is to reach that standard, not destroy it, lower it, or wiggle around it. In essence, reaching that standard means to become like Jesus. And according to 1 Peter 5:10, 11, it is only in the context of grace that God can perfect our characters.

Ellen White agreed.

> The followers of Christ are to become like Him—by the grace of God to form characters in harmony with the principles of His holy law. This is Bible sanctification.
>
> This work can be accomplished only through faith in Christ, by the power of the indwelling Spirit of God. . . . The Christian will feel the promptings of sin, but he will maintain a constant warfare against it. Here is where Christ's help is needed. Human weakness becomes united to divine strength, and faith exclaims, "Thanks be to God, which giveth us the victory through our Lord Jesus Christ." 1 Corinthians 15:57.[31]

Theodore Roosevelt once remarked, "The greatest victories are yet to be won. The greatest deeds are yet to be done." This is certainly true in the life of the person who fully surrenders his heart to King Jesus.

There is only one safe union to join. It is the Divine Human Union. Humanity was united with divinity in the person of Jesus Christ. Through the power of His Father that He received by faith, the God-Man "condemned sin in the flesh" (Romans 8:3). As our Elder Brother, Jesus concludes the Laodicean message with this call: "To him who overcomes I will grant to sit with Me on My throne, as I also overcame and sat down with My Father on His throne" (Revelation 3:22). As Jesus overcame through faith in His Father, we also can overcome "through faith in Christ, by the power of the indwelling Spirit of God." Praise His name!

Here is a powerful summary of the only way to receive righteousness, and of the failure of the Jewish nation. The warning is for us.

> While the law is holy, the Jews could not attain righteousness by their own efforts to keep the law. The disciples of Christ must obtain righteousness of a different character from that of the Pharisees, if they would enter the kingdom of heaven. God offered them, in His Son, the perfect righteousness of the law. If they would open their hearts fully to receive Christ, then the very life of God, His love, would dwell in them, transforming them into His own likeness; and thus through God's free

gift they would possess the righteousness which the law requires. But the Pharisees rejected Christ; being ignorant of God's righteousness, and going about to establish their own (Romans 10:3), they would not submit unto the righteousness of God.[32]

The third angel's message concludes with, "Here is the patience of the saints; here are those who keep the commandments of God and the faith of Jesus" (Revelation 14:12). Ellen White wrote,

> Elder E. J. Waggoner had the privilege granted him of speaking plainly and presenting his views upon justification by faith and the righteousness of Christ in relation to the law. This was no new light, but it was old light placed where it should be in the third angel's message.[33]

Understood in the context of the righteousness of Christ, we discover that the only way to really keep the commandments of God is by fully surrendering our hearts to Jesus and through justification by faith.

Paul wrote to early Christians in Rome, "The kingdom of God is not eating and drinking, but righteousness and peace and joy in the Holy Spirit" (Romans 14:17). Two years after Minneapolis, Ellen White's article, "The Righteousness of Christ," appeared in *The Review and Herald*. There she affirmed that the righteousness noted in the third angel's message, which is "keeping the commandments of God," comes alone through full heart surrender to the Savior. "God has lifted up His own standard,—the commandments of God and the faith of Jesus; and the experience that follows complete surrender to God, is righteousness, peace, and joy in the Holy Ghost."[34]

Isaiah wrote, "He has clothed me with the garments of salvation, He has covered me with the robe of righteousness" (Isaiah 61:10). This robe is more than a mere covering over of past transgressions. In Scripture, a "garment" or clothing also refers to character qualities inside a person. Peter exhorts the saints, "Be clothed with humility" (1 Peter 5:5). Concerning a wicked man, David lamented, "He clothed himself with cursing as with his garment" (Psalm 109:18). "Therefore," wrote Paul to believers, "put on tender mercies, kindness, humility, meekness, longsuffering. . . . But above all these things put on love" (Colossians 3:12–14). Thus the "clothing" of righteousness, humility, and love represents the character of Jesus that is imparted to us when we fully surrender ourselves to Him.

In her chapter, "Without a Wedding Garment," Ellen White gave this insightful summary:

> When we submit ourselves to Christ, the heart is united with His

heart, the will is submerged in His will, the mind becomes one with His mind, the thoughts are brought into captivity to Him; we live His life. This is what it means to be clothed with the garment of His righteousness. Then as the Lord looks upon us He sees, not the fig-leaf garment, not the nakedness and deformity of sin, but His own robe of righteousness, which is perfect obedience to the law of Jehovah.[35]

Then comes this solemn warning:Those who reject the gift of Christ's righteousness are rejecting the attributes of character which would constitute them the sons and daughters of God. They are rejecting that which alone could give them a fitness for a place at the marriage feast.[36]

Paul wrote, "Put on the Lord Jesus Christ" (Romans 13:14). Two friends went for a boat ride. The river was swift and deep, and the boat turned over. The owner of the vessel had taken two life jackets along. He later said, "I put mine on, but my buddy laid his down beside him. When we were unexpectedly tossed into the river, my life jacket brought me to the surface, but my friend never came up again." Oh friend, we must "put on" Jesus Christ, our Life Jacket. The gift of His character and life must become a part of our experience. If it doesn't, we will sink and drown in turbulent waters.

In 1893, A. T. Jones relayed this experience about the Minneapolis message and Christ's robe of righteousness:

A sister told me not long ago that before that time four years ago she had just been lamenting her estate, and wondering how in the world the time was ever going to come for the Lord to come, if He had to wait for His people to get ready to meet Him. For she said the way she had been at it—and she had worked as hard as anybody in this world, she thought—she saw that she was not making progress fast enough to bring the Lord in any reasonable time at all; and she could not make out how the Lord was going to come.

She was bothered about it; but she said when the folks came home from Minneapolis and they said, "Why the Lord's righteousness is a gift, we can have the righteousness of Christ as a gift, and we can have it now." "O," said she, "That made me glad; that brought light; for then I could see how the Lord could come pretty soon. When He Himself gives us the garment, the clothing, the character, that fits us for the judgment and for the time of trouble, I could then see how He could come just as soon as He wanted to." "And," said she, "it made me glad, and I have been glad ever since." Brethren, I am glad of it too, all the time.[37]

Me too!

Thus the third angel's message is a living thing, resulting in a living Savior, through the Holy Spirit, living in the hearts of God's people. Jesus left this earth nearly two thousand years ago, but when He ascended to heaven,

> the sense of His presence was still with His followers. It was a personal presence, full of love and light. . . . The light, and love, and power of the indwelling Christ shone out through them, so that men, beholding, "marveled; and they took knowledge of them, that they had been with Jesus" (Acts 4:13). All that Christ was to the disciples, He desires to be to His children today.[38]

In 1893, Elder Jones said to the delegates, "That is what we need to understand now, and know we understand it, before we start to give the third angel's message. . . . Let us have the third angel's message, which is the gospel of Jesus Christ."[39]

A wealthy businessman once took his six-year-old daughter to an art gallery in Washington, D.C. As they walked through the aisles, the little girl noticed a famous painting of Jesus knocking on the door of a house.

"Daddy, who is that?" the child asked.

"Why, that man's name is Jesus Christ," the father answered.

"What is He doing?" the girl wondered.

"I guess He is knocking on the door of someone's heart."

Thinking for a moment, the child questioned. "Why don't people let Him come in?"

A bit uneasy, the man responded, "I guess because things get in the way."

Captivated by the picture, the little girl then asked her father, "What things?"

"Oh, probably things like money, or nice things, or even some friends."

The man walked on. But when he looked back, he discovered that his daughter had not moved. She stood still, staring at the picture. Then he noticed a tear form in her eyes and trickle down her cheek. "Honey, why are you crying?" he asked.

The little girl then turned to her father and moaned softly, "Oh, Daddy, have you let Jesus come in?"

Dear friend, how about you? Have you let Jesus come in? He loves you, and He is knocking on the door of your heart right now. His Presence on the Inside will give you more peace than you can possibly imagine.

In spite of his riches, rock singer Mick Jagger still sings his popular song, "I can't get no satisfaction." Whether Mick knows it or not, the real reason for his lack is that he does not know Jesus the Savior.

It is only through a centered-in-the-cross understanding of the third angel's message that true satisfaction can be found. It is the love of Jesus Christ alone that can satisfy our deepest longings. His personal presence is the only hope for our shattered world.

Oh friend, have *you* let Jesus come in?

---

1. White, *Steps to Christ,* 51.
2. White, *Testimonies to Ministers,* 91.
3. White, *Mount of Blessing,* 114.
4. *Signs of the Times,* September 8, 1892.
5. White, *Testimonies to Ministers,* 92.
6. White, *Steps to Christ,* 18.
7. Ibid., 62.
8. Ibid., 52.
9. *1893 General Conference Bulletin,* 264.
10. White, *Steps to Christ,* 52.
11. White, *Steps to Christ,* 20.
12. White, *Mount of Blessing,* 18.
13. White, *Testimonies to Ministers,* 91.
14. *The Review and Herald,* April 1, 1890.
15. White, *Steps to Christ,* 57.
16. *1893 General Conference Bulletin,* 263.
17. White, *Steps to Christ,* 61.
18. *Signs of the Times,* September 8, 1892.
19. *Signs of the Times,* September 22, 1890.
20. White, *Steps to Christ,* 60.
21. Ibid., 61.
22. Ibid.
23. Ibid., 60.
24. White, *Testimonies to Ministers,* 92.
25. White, *Patriarchs and Prophets,* 64.
26. *The Review and Herald,* September 3, 1889.
27. White, *The Desire of Ages,* 671.
28. Ibid., 311.
29. White, *Testimonies to Ministers,* 91.
30. *Signs of the Times,* July 14, 1890.
31. White, *The Great Controversy,* 469.
32. White, *Mount of Blessing,* 54, 55.
33. *1888 Materials,* 211, 212.
34. *The Review and Herald,* August 19, 1890.

35. White, *Christ's Object Lessons,* 312.
36. Ibid., 316, 317.
37. *1893 General Conference Bulletin,* 361.
38. White, *Steps to Christ,* 73, 74.
39. *1893 General Conference Bulletin,* 263.

CHAPTER FIFTEEN

PUTTING THE PIECES TOGETHER

"THE INFORMATION IS OUT THERE.
YOU JUST HAVE TO SEPARATE THE FACTS FROM WIVES' TALES."
—Attributed to Larry Rogers

The third angel's message, which contains Heaven's last message to our fallen world, teaches "the commandments of God and the faith of Jesus" (Revelation 14:12). Correctly understood, it is a Spirit-filled combining of the Ten Commandments and the gospel of God's free grace. Jesus Christ is the center of the message. Its focus is what He has done on the cross for all humanity, and what He can do inside every soul who fully surrenders and trusts in Him.

The following clear and distinct summaries were written more than a hundred years ago by the key players in this drama of cosmic significance. Read them carefully. Compare them with your Bible. Then strengthen yourself—not in speculative fantasy, foolishness, or carefully crafted satanic detours, but with the truth of the living God.

From E. J. Waggoner:

> Let the reader try to picture the scene. Here stands the law as the swift witness against the sinner. It cannot change, and it will not call the sinner a righteous man. The convicted sinner tries again and again to obtain righteousness from the law, but it resists all his advances. It cannot be bribed by any amount of penance or professedly good deeds. But here stands Christ, "full of grace," as well as of truth, calling the sinner to Him. At last the sinner, weary of the vain struggle to get righteousness from the law, listens to the voice of Christ, and flees to His outstretched arms. Hiding in Christ, he is covered with righteousness;

and now behold! he has obtained through faith in Christ, the righteousness for which he has been vainly striving. He has the righteousness which the law requires, and it is the genuine article, because he obtained it from the Source of Righteousness; from the very place whence the law came.[1]

Another from E. J. Waggoner:

And now for a very brief summary of the verses that we have commented upon. First, all are guilty, condemned by the law, so that they cannot get from it the righteousness which it requires. They try again and again, but in vain; they cannot turn aside its just condemnation. But now Christ appears on the scene. He is the one whence the law derives all its righteousness, and He promises to give it freely to all who accept it. This He can do, because grace, as well as truth, comes by Him. The sinner accepts Christ, tremblingly, yet knowing that it is his only hope. Christ covers him with the robe of righteousness (Isaiah 61:10) and puts His righteousness into his heart. He takes away the filthy garment, and clothes him with a change of raiment, saying, "Behold, I have caused thine iniquity to pass from thee" (Zechariah 3:3-5).[2]

From A. T. Jones:

And thus, just as our sins actually committed were imputed to Him, that His righteousness might be imputed to us; so His meeting and conquering, in the flesh, the liability to sin, and in the same flesh manifesting righteousness, enables us in Him, and Him in us, to meet and conquer in the flesh this same liability to sin, and to manifest righteousness in the same flesh. And thus it is that for the sins which we have actually committed, for the sins that are past, His righteousness is imputed to us, as our sins were imputed to Him. And to keep us from sinning, His righteousness is imparted to us in our flesh; as our flesh, with its liability to sin, was imparted to Him. Thus He is a complete Savior. He saves from all sins that we have actually committed; and saves equally from all the sins that we might commit, dwelling apart from Him.[3]

From R. T. Nash, an eyewitness at Minneapolis:

The writer of this little tract attended the Minneapolis conference in 1888 and saw and heard many of the various things that were done and said. Mrs. E.G. White from California was present, also Dr. E.J. Waggoner and Elder Alonzo T Jones from California were there. It fell to the lot of Jones and Waggoner to conduct each morning the consecration services of the conference. They taught us in the most kind and simple way that Jesus the Lamb of God took upon Himself all our burden of sin and gave His life for us. That He paid the whole debt and set us free. That He took all our sins and in exchange gave us His righteousness. That He took our filthy robes and gave us the white robe of His righteousness in its place. What a wonderful exchange! "If we confess our sins, He is faithful and just to forgive us our sins, and to cleanse us from all unrighteousness" (1 John 1:9). "Being then made free from sin," (Romans 6:10) "the gift of righteousness" (Romans 5:17) is ours by faith.[4]

From Ellen White:

> The Lord in His great mercy sent a most precious message to His people through Elders Waggoner and Jones. This message was to bring more prominently before the world the uplifted Savior, the sacrifice for the sins of the whole world. It presented justification through faith in the Surety; it invited the people to receive the righteousness of Christ, which is made manifest in obedience to all the commandments of God. Many had lost sight of Jesus. They needed to have their eyes directed to His divine person, His merits, and His changeless love for the human family. All power is given unto His hands, that He may dispense rich gifts to men, imparting the priceless gift of His own righteousness to the helpless human agent. This is the message that God commanded to be given to the world, it is the third angel's message, which is to be proclaimed with a loud voice, and attended with the outpouring of His Spirit in a large measure. . . . This is the testimony that must go throughout the length and breadth of the world. It presents the law and the gospel, binding up the two in a perfect whole.[5]

The final summary from *Steps to Christ* is, to me, the clearest of them all. My comments are in brackets, based on what we have studied:

> Righteousness is defined [the biblical definition, see Psalm 119:172] by the standard of God's holy law, as expressed in the ten precepts given on Sinai. . . . It was possible for Adam, before the fall, to form a righteous character by obedience to God's law. But He failed to do this, and because of his sin our natures are fallen and we cannot make ourselves righteous.

Since we are sinful, unholy, we cannot perfectly obey the holy law. We have no righteousness of our own with which to meet the claims of the law of God [our helpless condition].

But Christ has made a way of escape for us. He lived on earth amid trials and temptations such as we have to meet. He lived a sinless life [His righteousness]. He died for us [the gospel of His grace], and now He offers to take our sins and give us His righteousness [His wonderful offer]. If you give yourself to Him [the simple condition], and accept Him as your Savior, then, sinful as your life may have been, for His sake you are accounted righteous. Christ's character stands in the place of your character, and you are accepted before God just as if you had not sinned [justification by faith and the imputed righteousness of Christ].

More than this, Christ changes the heart [sanctification]. He abides in your heart by faith [the imparted righteousness of Christ]. You are to maintain this connection with Christ by faith and the continual surrender of your will to Him [a daily experience of total dependence on Christ] and so long as you do this, He will work in you to will and to do according to His good pleasure. So you may say, "The life which I now live in the flesh I live by the faith of the Son of God, who loved me [His love motivates], and gave Himself for me" (Galatians 2:20). So Jesus said to His disciples, "It is not ye that speak, but the Spirit of your Father which speaketh in you" (Matthew 10:20).

Then with Christ working in you [the secret of power], you will manifest the same spirit and do the same good works, works of righteousness [all righteousness comes from Jesus], obedience [the true test]. So we have nothing of ourselves of which to boast [all pride comes from Satan]. Our only ground of hope is in the righteousness of Christ imputed to us [justification by faith] and in that wrought by His Spirit working in and through us [the imparted righteousness of Christ].

But when we speak of faith, there is a distinction that should be borne in mind. There is a kind of belief that is wholly distinct from faith. The existence and power of God, the truth of His word, are facts that even Satan and his hosts cannot at heart deny. The Bible says, "the devils also believe, and tremble;" but this is not faith. James 2:19. Where there is not only a belief in God's Word, but a submission of the will to Him; where the heart is yielded to Him, the affections fixed upon Him, there is faith—faith that works by love and purifies the soul [true faith which works]. Through this faith the heart is renewed in the image of God. And the heart that in its unrenewed state is not subject to the law of God, neither indeed can be, now delights in its holy precepts, exclaiming with the Psalmist, "O how I love Thy law! It is my meditation all the day" (Psalm 119:97). And the righteousness of the law might be fulfilled in us, "who walk not after the flesh, but after the Spirit" (Romans 8:1).[6]

A wealthy American businessman once toured China. Needing to cross a certain river, he hired a poor Chinese man to take him across in his small boat. As the poor man rowed, the haughty businessman asked, "Do you know what the largest country in the world is?"

"No," the uneducated man replied.

"How about the longest river?" the rich man asked sarcastically.

"Sorry," the poor man said again.

"What about the tallest mountain?"

"Can't say that I do." The rich man felt so superior. But halfway across the river, a storm suddenly burst upon them. As the little boat began filling up with water, the businessman started to panic. Now it was the Chinese man's turn to ask a question. "Do you know how to swim?"

"No!" the rich man blurted out as their boat began to sink. That rich man knew many things, except the one thing that would keep him alive.

God's Last Message: Christ Our Righteousness is the only message that can keep our souls alive forever. If we refuse to learn it, and to experience it, there is a good chance we will finally sink hopelessly into "the lake of fire" (Revelation 20:15).

The American flag is red, white, and blue, which might also be considered the colors of the third angel's message. Red is for washing in the blood of Christ. White is for the robe of His righteousness. True blue is for obedience to the Ten Commandments, through faith in Jesus. Shall we not stand under His bloodstained banner and wave the flag of truth for all the world to see?

---

1. Waggoner, *Christ and His Righteousness,* 62.

2. *Signs of the Times,* September 8, 1890.

3. Alonzo Trévier Jones, *The Consecrated Way* (Mountain View, CA: Pacific Press®, 1905), 42, 43.

4. *Manuscripts and Memories of Minneapolis 1888,* 352–354.

5. White, *Testimonies to Ministers,* 91, 92, 94.

6. White, *Steps to Christ,* 61–63.

CHAPTER SIXTEEN

1889 REVIVALS SPEAK TODAY

"HISTORY IS A BETTER GUIDE THAN GOOD INTENTIONS."
—Jeane Kirkpatrick (1926–2006), U.S. Ambassador to the United Nations

Shortly after the Minneapolis meeting in 1888, A. T. Jones, E. J. Waggoner, and Ellen White went on a gospel tour, speaking at camp meetings and in churches. Tremendous revivals occurred, and this will soon be duplicated as the same message is experienced and preached from the Bible in these last days. The following reports from the pen of Ellen White can be found in Review and Herald articles published throughout 1889.

February 1889:

> Revival Work in the Battle Creek Church—Elds. A. T. Jones, J. O. Corless, and others took an active part in conducting the meetings. The principal topic dwelt upon was justification by faith, and this truth came as meat in due season to the people of God. The living oracles of God were presented in new and precious light. . . . They expressed their gladness and gratitude of heart for the sermons that had been preached by Bro. A. T. Jones; they saw the truth, goodness, mercy and love of God as they never before had seen it. They humbled their hearts, confessed their sins, and removed everything that had separated their souls from God, and the Lord put a new song into their mouths, even praises to His name. . . . There were many who testified that they were free in the Lord,—not free from temptation; for they had these to contend with every day,—but they believed their sins were forgiven.[1]

March 1889:

Meetings at South Lancaster, Mass.—Elder Jones came from Boston, and labored most earnestly for the people, speaking twice and sometimes three times a day. . . . There were many who testified that as the searching truths had been presented, they had been convicted in the light of the law as transgressors. They had been trusting in their own righteousness. Now they saw it as filthy rags, in comparison with the righteousness of Christ, which is alone acceptable to God. While they had not been open transgressors, they saw themselves depraved and degraded in heart. They had substituted other gods in the place of their Heavenly Father. They had struggled to refrain from sin, but had trusted in their own strength.

We should go to Jesus just as we are, confess our sins, and cast our helpless souls upon our compassionate Redeemer. This subdues the pride of heart, and is a crucifixion of self. . . . The deep movings of the Spirit of God have been felt upon almost every heart. The general testimony was borne by those who attended the meeting that they had obtained an experience beyond anything they had known before. . . . I have never seen a revival work go forward with such thoroughness.[2]

July 1889:

Camp-Meeting at Ottawa, Kansas—Brn. A. T. and D. T. Jones, and others, had wrought perseveringly to impress the people with the truth. . . . On Sabbath, truths were presented that were new to the majority of the congregation. . . . Light flashed from the oracles of God in relation to the law and the gospel, in relation to the fact that Christ is our righteousness, which seemed to souls who were hungry for the truth, as light too precious to be received. . . . One brother spoke of the struggle that he had experienced before he could receive the good news that Christ is our righteousness. . . . The Lord presented the truth before him in clear lines, revealing the fact that Christ alone is the source of all hope and salvation. . . .

One of our young ministering brethren said that he had enjoyed more of the blessing and love of God during that meeting than in all his life before. . . . [Another] saw that it was his privilege to be justified by faith; he had peace with God, and with tears confessed what relief and blessing had come to his soul. . . . We thank the Lord with all the heart that we have precious light to present before the people, and we rejoice that we have a message for this time which is present truth. The tidings that Christ is our righteousness has brought relief to many, many souls. . . . In every meeting since the General Conference, souls have eagerly accepted the precious message of the righteousness of Christ.[3]

August 1889:

> Camp-Meeting at Williamsport, PA.—The message was eagerly welcomed. . . . The Lord has worked for His people, and they have received the light with joy as meat in due season. . . . The churches in Pennsylvania have been passing through discouragements, and some of their members have apostatized. But as the precious message of present truth was spoken to the people by Brn. Jones and Waggoner, the people saw new beauty in the third angel's message, and they were greatly encouraged. They testified to the fact that they had never before attended meetings where they had received so much instruction and such precious light.[4]

September 1889:

> Camp-Meeting at Rome, N.Y.—The present message, justification by faith— is a message from God; it bears the divine credentials, for its fruit is unto holiness . . . The doctrine of justification by faith was presented at the Rome meeting, it came to many as water comes to the thirsty traveler. . . . If the enemy of truth and righteousness can obliterate from the mind the thought that it is necessary to depend upon the righteousness of Christ for salvation, he will do it. If Satan can lead man to place value upon his own works as works of merit and righteousness, he knows that he can overcome him by his temptations, and make him his victim and prey. Lift up Jesus before the people. Strike the doorposts with the blood of Calvary's Lamb, and you are safe.[5]

Looking back with delight in the year 1890, Ellen White gave these marvelous summaries of those wonderful revival meetings:

> I have traveled from place to place, attending meetings where the message of the righteousness of Christ was preached. I consider it a privilege to stand by the side of my brethren, and give my testimony with the message for this time; and 1 saw the power of God attend the message wherever it was spoken. You could not make the people believe in South Lancaster that it was not a message of light that came to them. The people confessed their sins, and appropriated the righteousness of Christ. God has set His hand to do this work. We labored in Chicago a week before there was a break in the meetings. But like a wave of glory,

the blessing of God swept over us as we pointed men to the Lamb of God that taketh away the sin of the world. The Lord revealed His glory, and we felt the deep movings of the Spirit. Everywhere the message led to the confession of sin, and to the putting away of iniquity.[6]

Brother Jones has borne the message from church to church, and from state to state; and light and freedom and the outpouring of the Spirit of God has attended the work.[7]

Finally, "Our churches are dying for the want of teaching on *the subject* of righteousness by faith in Christ, and for kindred truths."[8]

Is it the same today?

---

1. *The Review and Herald,* February 12, 1889.
2. *The Review and Herald,* March 5, 1889.
3. *The Review and Herald,* July 23, 1889. The last line of this quote exposes the error of those who state categorically that the Seventh-day Adventist Church rejected the message of Jones and Waggoner.
4. *The Review and Herald,* August 13, 1889.
5. *The Review and Herald,* September 3, 1889.
6. *The Review and Herald,* March 18, 1890.
7. Letter, January 9, 1893.
8. *The Review and Herald,* March 25, 1890.

CHAPTER SEVENTEEN

THE COMING 18.88
EARTHQUAKE

"DON'T HOLD ONTO THE PAST. THE FUTURE HOLDS MORE PROMISE."
—Attributed to Josh Holman

On Friday, March 11, 2011, one of the strongest earthquakes ever recorded
struck off the coast of Japan, killing more than 15,000 people, creating a
133-foot tsunami, and crippling three nuclear reactors. The shock even caused
planet Earth to shift on its axis.

I grew up on the opposite end of the Pacific Ocean, in the Hollywood Hills
of Southern California. Many earthquakes occur in this region too, and a deep
fear exists among many Los Angeles residents that someday soon the Big One
will strike there too, most likely along the San Andreas fault.

I hope not, for many of my closest relatives live in L.A. But I do know that
in a spiritual sense, another gigantic tremor is coming, much larger than 9.03
quake that rocked Japan. When it comes to revivals, it will definitely be the Big
One, and its holy power will be felt around the world. The book of Revelation
describes it this way: "After these things I saw another angel coming down from
heaven, having great authority, and the earth was illuminated with his glory"
(Revelation 18:1).

This word has come to us that

before the final visitation of God's judgments upon the earth there will
be among the people of the Lord such a revival of primitive godliness as
has not been witnessed since apostolic times. The Spirit and power of

God will be poured out upon His children.[1]

Faithful Seventh-day Adventists and godly Christians of other denominations everywhere long for this revival, this Pentecost II. The above quote from *The Great Controversy* comes from an insightful chapter called "Modern Revivals." A careful examination of that chapter reveals that, just as the plates on the San Andreas fault can clash together to produce an earthquake, so the coming together of the law of God and the gospel of Jesus Christ will produce the final revival predicted in Revelation 18:1.

> The nature and the importance of the law of God have been, to a great extent, lost sight of. A wrong conception of the character, the perpetuity, and the obligation of the divine law has led to errors in relation to conversion and sanctification, and has resulted in lowering the standard of piety in the church. Mere is to be found the secret of the lack of the Spirit and the power of God in the revivals of our time.[2]

> From the habit of underrating the divine law and justice, the extent and demerit of human disobedience, men easily slide into the habit of underestimating the grace which has provided an atonement for sin. Thus the gospel loses its value and importance in the minds of men.[3]

Notice carefully: "It is only as the law of God is restored to its rightful position [as a schoolmaster leading to Christ] that there can be a revival of primitive faith and godliness among His professed people."[4] Obviously, the "great earthquake" of the final revival cannot occur without the preaching of the gospel of Jesus Christ. But neither will doomed sinners be able to appreciate the value of the gospel without an awareness of their sins, which comes from the law. Ellen White clarified:

> The law without faith in the gospel of Christ cannot save the transgressor. The gospel without the law is inefficient and powerless. . . . The two blended—the gospel of Christ and the law of God—produce the love and faith unfeigned.[5]

If we want God's love to be produced in our hearts "which is made manifest in keeping all the commandments of God" then the law and the gospel *must* be united in our preaching and in our experience. "If we would have the spirit and power of the third angel's message, we *must* present the law and the gospel together, for they go hand in hand."[6] When these mighty plates (the law and the gospel) finally come together one last time just before the end of the world, the resulting earthquake will register 18.88 on God's spiritual Richter scale. When that happens, this revival will shake the world.

Satan fears this quake.

But just as those poor inhabitants of Japan couldn't stop the March 11, 2011 catastrophe, ultimately, neither can the devil stop the coming shaking. His tricks may hinder it for a time, but eventually it "will come and will not tarry" (Hebrews 10:37).

Let's be ready for it.

---

1. White, *The Great Controversy*, 464.
2. Ibid., 465.
3. Ibid., 466.
4. Ibid., 478.
5. *1888 Materials*, 783.
6. Ellen G. White, *Gospel Workers*, 161.

CHAPTER EIGHTEEN

WARNING: SATANIC DETOURS ARE HAZARDOUS TO YOUR HEALTH

"SELF-DECEPTION REMAINS THE MOST DIFFICULT DECEPTION."
—Joan Didion (1934–), U.S. essayist

Just as in 1888, Satan is now working desperately to prevent "this truth" of the law of God and the gospel of Christ's righteousness from receiving prominence and priority among the Lord's people. The devil has many false signposts set up all along the highway to the Holy City calculated to get us off track. A thousand side roads read, "This Way." As a sign on countless other gospels, the word *Detour* appears in neon lights. With subtle satanic trickery, the Prince of Darkness sets up another bold sign stating, "Danger. Falling Rocks Ahead," right in front of the truth. God warned, "There is a way that seems right to a man, but its end is the way of death" (Proverbs 14:12). That proverb has never been truer than it is today.

This is the Age of Counterfeits.

But as we approach the grand finale, the Maker of heaven and earth is once again moving mightily so that His true message will take the field.

> As a power from beneath is stirring up the children of disobedience to make void the law of God, and to trample on the truth that Christ is our righteousness, a power from above is moving upon the hearts of those who are loyal, to exalt the law, and to lift up Jesus as a complete Savior.[1]

The battle is on. The stakes are high.
The issues are life and death.

> Satan is wide-awake, and is studying and counseling with his angels
> another mode of attack where he can be successful. The contest will wax
> more and more fierce on the part of Satan; for he is moved by a power
> from beneath. As the work of God's people moves forward with sanc-
> tified, resistless energy, planting the standard of Christ's righteousness
> in the church, moved by a power from the throne of God, the great
> controversy will wax stronger and stronger, and become more and more
> determined. Mind will be arrayed against mind, plans against plans,
> principles of heavenly origin against principles of Satan. Truth in its
> varied phases will be in conflict with error in its ever-varying, increasing
> forms, and which, if possible, will deceive the very elect.[2]

At the conclusion of a chapter titled, "Rejecting the Light," Ellen White
gave a solemn warning to those who were resisting the third angel's message
centered in the righteousness of Christ as preached by Jones and Waggoner
during the Minneapolis era. The warning is for us.

> If you reject Christ's delegated messengers, you reject Christ. Neglect
> this great salvation, kept before you for years, despise the glorious offer
> of justification through the blood of Christ and sanctification through
> the cleansing power of the Holy Spirit, and there remaineth no more
> sacrifice for sins, but a certain fearful looking for of judgment and fi-
> ery indignation. I entreat you now to humble yourselves and cease your
> stubborn resistance of light and evidence. Say unto the Lord, Mine in-
> iquities have separated between me and my God. O Lord, pardon my
> transgressions. Blot out my sins from the book of Thy remembrance.
> Praise His holy name, there is forgiveness with Him, and you can be
> converted, transformed.[3]

In rejecting the message given at Minneapolis, *men committed sin.*[4]

> The time will come when many will be willing to do anything and
> everything possible in order to have a chance of hearing the call which
> they rejected at Minneapolis. God moved upon their hearts, but many
> yielded to another spirit, which was moving upon their passions from
> beneath.[5]

Let's not repeat the history of some of our misguided forefathers. In these final times we need the full benefits of the message sent from heaven. The hour is too late to follow even one of Satan's false signposts, unbalanced ideas, extremist notions, and delusional messages. If we are ensnared by his devices, take a wrong turn, and miss "the special power of the Holy Spirit" that comes from uniting the law and the gospel, the result will be disastrous. Notice carefully:

> Unless divine power is brought into the experience of the people of God, false theories and ideas will take minds captive, Christ and His righteousness will be dropped out of the experience of many, and their faith will be without power or life.[6]

Will we heed the warning?

---

1. White, *Gospel Workers,* 161.
2. White, *Testimonies to Ministers,* 407.
3. Ibid., 97, 98.
4. *1888 Materials,* 913.
5. Ibid., 1030, 1031.
6. White, *Gospel Workers,* 162.

CHAPTER NINETEEN

A White Robe for Naked Laodiceans

"WE RISE IN GLORY AS WE SINK IN PRIDE."

—Andrew Young (1932–), American politician, diplomat, activist, and pastor

To the angel of the church of the Laodiceans," declared Jesus Christ to John, "write . . ." (Revelation 3:14). The word *Laodicea* literally means, "A people judged." The Laodicean message is now being given to God's professed end-time church during this "hour of His judgment" (Revelation 14:7). "These things says the Amen, the Faithful and True Witness, the Beginning of the creation of God" (Revelation 3:14). Jesus Christ Himself is the True Witness. He sees what lies hidden in the depths of human hearts. Motivated by love, He sends this warning to His professed people: "You are neither cold nor hot. I could wish you were cold or hot. So then, because you are lukewarm, and neither cold nor hot, I will vomit you out of My mouth" (Revelation 3:15, 16).

The root problem with Laodicean Christians is a subtle form of spiritual pride. Laodiceans do not actually proclaim out loud, "I am rich . . ." but this thought lurks inside their heads. Addressing the same issue, Jesus once told a parable about a wealthy man who "thought within himself, saying" (Luke 12:17). Isaiah wrote concerning Satan, "You have said in your heart: 'I will ascend into heaven' " (Isaiah 14:13). Babylon also "says in her heart, 'I sit as queen' " (Revelation 18:7). It's the same with Laodicea. The root problem isn't obvious even to Laodiceans themselves but entirely mental and hidden.

I once saw a billboard on the side of an interstate highway promot-ing the U.S. Navy. The primary image on the sign was a submarine silently maneuvering far below the surface. In bold letters, the caption read, "Our Pride Runs Deep." Those words impressed me. I then thought about Satan, Laodicea, and Babylon.

Deep-seated pride is the root problem, I concluded.

The "I am rich and increased with goods" statement spoken deep in the heart of Laodiceans in Revelation 3:17 is actually a quote from the Old Testament book of Hosea. "Ephraim said, 'Surely I have become rich, I have found wealth for myself; in all my labors they shall find in me no iniquity that is sin' " (Hosea 12:8). With spiritual smugness, Ephraim concluded that God would "find . . . no iniquity" in her. Yet the True Witness discerned the truth deep down beneath the surface. After an objective examination, God's sentence was pronounced: "Their heart was exalted; therefore they forgot Me" (Hosea 13:6).

When Satan's "heart was lifted up," the Lord told him, "iniquity was found in you" (Ezekiel 28:17, 15). Today, Satan's self-exalting spirit leads many a man to "to think of himself more highly than he ought to think" (Romans 12:3). Pride is natural to our fallen human nature. Yet it is sin, as God says, "Look, this was the iniquity of your sister Sodom: She and her daughter had pride" (Ezekiel 16:49). Laodicea's pride is sin too, and "sin is lawlessness" (1 John 3:4). Out of "the midst of the fire" on Mt. Sinai, God commanded, "You shall have no other gods before Me" (Exodus 20:3). But for those dwelling in a dark, Laodicean, delusional dreamland, self has become "another god" above Jesus Christ.

As with ancient Ephraim, so it is with God's professed end-time Laodicean church. "His sin is bound up" (Hosea 13:12). With psychology's current obsession about "feeling good" about oneself, it has become even more difficult for sinners to see their soul poverty. But the Amen sees everything. In mercy He lifts the veil and testifies, "Do you not know that you are wretched, miserable, poor, blind, and naked?" (Revelation 3:17). Naked Laodiceans are *not* clothed with the righteousness of Jesus Christ. They are "without a wedding garment" (Matthew 22:12). Those in this condition "do not appropriate the righteousness of Christ; it is a robe unworn by them, a fullness unknown, a fountain untouched."[1] The deception is deep, dark, and deadly.

> Were you cold, there would be some hope that you would be converted, but where self-righteousness girds one about, instead of the righteousness of Christ, the deception is so difficult to be seen, and the self-righteousness so hard to put away, that the case of the sinner is difficult to reach.[2]

But the Spirit of God is trying hard. Right now, around the world, the third angel is proclaiming with a loud voice "the commandments of God and the faith of Jesus." The powerful, no-compromise, soul-healing medicinal blend of the law of God and the gospel of Jesus Christ is the only hope for those who mistakenly think they "have need of nothing" (Revelation 3:17). But as we approach the glory and terrors of Sinai and hear heaven's Almighty King thundering from His mountain pulpit, we find that "the law reveals sin to us, and causes us to feel our need of Christ and to flee unto Him for pardon and peace by exercising repentance toward God and faith toward our Lord Jesus Christ."[3] One glimpse of "the Lord sitting on a throne, high and lifted up" (Isaiah 6:1) humbles all human pride into the dust. One ray of light from "the Lord our Righteousness" reveals the sinful depths of every iota of human self-righteousness. With eyes anointed with heavenly eye salve we finally discern "the shame of [our] nakedness" (Revelation 3:18). Then we will cry out with the unworthy tax collector, "God, be merciful to me a sinner!" (Luke 18:13).

Ah, perfect!

This is exactly the Lord's plan.

Jesus speaks tenderly to those thus stricken, "I counsel you to buy from Me . . . white garments, that you may be clothed." Amazing love! Jesus offers to place over our naked life the white garments of His own spotless righteousness. "As many as I love," the Good Shepherd declares, "I rebuke and chasten. Therefore be zealous and repent" (Revelation 3:19). As the Holy Spirit reveals to our darkened minds the mangled form of a slain Lamb crucified because of all our Laodicean pride, we are led to the foot of the cross in repentance for the sins that broke the heart of the Son of God.

> When we behold the great love of God, selfishness appears to us in its hideous and repulsive character, and we desire to have it expelled from the soul. As the Holy Spirit glorifies Christ, our hearts are softened and subdued, the temptation loses its power, and the grace of Christ transforms the character.[4]

Isn't grace powerful?

Jesus said, "He who humbles himself will be exalted" (Luke 18:14). Again, "Blessed are the poor in spirit, for theirs is the kingdom of heaven" (Matthew 5:3). During World War II, American soldiers went through heavy training in boot camps. One drill required them to crawl quickly across the ground underneath a wire just above their heads. Live bullets whizzed above the wire.

To survive, they needed to stay low.

So do we. Those who remain low in humility will "grow in . . . grace" (2 Peter 3:18). Those too high will die.

> The lower we lie at the foot of the cross the more clear will be our

view of Christ. For just as soon as we begin to lift ourselves up and to think that we are something, the view of Christ grows dimmer and dimmer and Satan steps in so that we cannot see Him at all.[5]

How frightening. Let's stay low so we can see Jesus. Those who "are clothed with the righteousness of Christ" will "have a humble estimate of themselves."[6] Someone once said, "God has two thrones: one in the highest heaven and the other in the lowliest heart."

Jesus continues, "Behold, I stand at the door and knock. If anyone hears My voice and opens the door, I will come in to him and dine with him, and he with Me" (Revelation 3:20). Here is the core of the Laodicean message.

> (It) is designed to arouse the people of God, to discover to them their backslidings, and to lead them to zealous repentance, that they might be favored with the presence of Jesus, and be fitted for the loud cry of the third angel.[7]

Only the presence of Jesus, who is "gentle and lowly in heart" (Matthew 11:29), has the power to cast King Self out of the soul temple. Christ alone can purify the heart as He "imparts the priceless gift of His own righteousness" to the surrendered, trusting believer.

Remember, Jesus Christ "is Lord" (Philippians 2:11), not you or me.

At the 1893 General Conference Session, A. T. Jones commented, "Who will be fitted for the loud cry of the third angel?—Those who have the presence of Jesus Christ. Those to whom the Laodicean message has brought by its working and by its intent, the presence of Jesus Christ."[8] Jones then quoted *Steps to Christ,* revealing how this "presence of Jesus" is "a personal presence, full of love and light."[9]

> His personal presence is to be with us. That is what the Laodicean message is to do for us; it brings the presence of Christ to live in us. . . . That is the righteousness of God, which is by faith of Jesus Christ.[10]

Thus the Judgment message (Revelation 14:7), the third angel's message (Revelation 14:9–12), and the Laodicean message (Revelation 3:14–22) all point to the imputed and imparted righteousness of Jesus Christ.

---

1. *The Review and Herald,* November 29, 1892.
2. White, *Testimonies to the Church,* 2:126.
3. White, *Selected Messages,* 1:234.

4. White, *Mount of Blessing,* 118.

5. *1888 Materials,* 159.

6. *The Review and Herald,* December 16, 1890.

7. White, *Testimonies to the Church,* 1:186.

8. *1893 General Conference Bulletin,* 297.

9. White, *Steps to Christ,* 73, 74.

10. *1893 General Conference Bulletin,* 300, 301.

CHAPTER TWENTY

THE FORGOTTEN MANUSCRIPT THAT SHAPED MINNEAPOLIS

"IS THERE IN THIS WORLD ANY MAN SO RESTRAINED BY HUMILITY THAT HE DOES NOT MIND REPROOF, AS A WELL-TRAINED HORSE THE WHIP?"
—Max Müller (1823–1900), German born British philologist and Sanskrit scholar

Both E. J. Waggoner and A. T. Jones experienced the practical application of the Laodicean message, and this prepared them to give the third angel's message. Many today are "running with a message," yet they have little idea of the nature of the preparation needed before they can give the message in the Spirit of Jesus Christ. Paul wrote to young Timothy, "Take heed to yourself and to the doctrine" (1 Timothy 4:16). A true messenger of God must first become "a vessel for honor, sanctified and useful for the Master, prepared for every good work" (2 Timothy 2:21).

In order to understand the deep spiritual preparation that occurred in the heart of Dr. Waggoner, it is essential that we understand what I have come to call "The Forgotten Manuscript That Shaped Minneapolis." To understand this manuscript, it is necessary to have some historical background of the controversy that took place in Adventist history concerning the law in Galatians.

Paul wrote that sinners are "not justified by the works of the law but by faith in Jesus Christ" (Galatians 2:16). Again, "The law was our tutor to bring us to Christ, that we might be justified by faith" (Galatians 3:24).

As Seventh-day Adventist ministers proclaimed the Ten Commandments in the 1860s, 1870s, and 1880s, including the fourth commandment about the seventh-day Sabbath (see Exodus 20:8–11), some Sunday-keeping pastors challenged them by saying, "Read Galatians! Don't you realize that New Testament Christians are not justified by the law, but by grace? *Therefore we don't need to keep the Sabbath.*" This argument is common today. At that time, the official Adventist response was, "Not so fast! The law Paul wrote about in Galatians is the ceremonial law, not the Big Ten; therefore we still need to keep the Sabbath."

Debates were intense. *The Review and Herald,* the official publication of the Seventh-day Adventist Church headquartered in Battle Creek, Michigan, took that latter position.

In the 1880s, E. J. Waggoner and A. T. Jones became co-editors of *Signs of the Times,* an Adventist journal published by Pacific Press® in California. In July–September 1886, Jones and Waggoner ran a nine-part series of articles called, "Comments on Galatians," which contended that the law in Galatians was not the ceremonial law but rather the Ten Commandments, as many non-Adventist challengers had argued.

But here's the catch. The Jones and Waggoner position was that the Big Ten, being still in force, pointed sinners to Jesus Christ, who through His death could justify man solely by His grace but who could also enable truly converted souls to keep the law.

Church leaders in Battle Creek felt threatened and concluded that the two upstart co-editors in California were actually weakening the basic Adventist mission to uphold the Ten Commandments. As a national Sunday law—introduced by Senator Blair into Congress on May 21, 1888[1]—loomed on the American horizon in the late 1800s, the Battle Creek brethren decided that their West Coast counterparts had unwittingly become party to a satanic plot calculated to undermine God's Law right before earth's final crisis, when "the mark of the beast" (see Revelation 19:20) would be enforced.

The result? Intense controversy.

G. I. Butler, president of the General Conference, favored the Battle Creek view that the law in Galatians was the ceremonial law and felt duty-bound to combat what he saw as a West Coast conspiracy spearheaded by Satan. In November of 1886, the Review and Herald Publishing Association published Butler's book, *The Law in the Book of Galatians: Is it the Moral Law, or Does it Refer to that System of Laws Peculiarly Jewish?* which countered Waggoner's and Jones's *Signs* articles. But the dynamic duo in California felt equally obligated to defend God's truth.

On February 10, 1887, Waggoner responded with his own book, *The Gospel in the Book of Galatians,* which countered Butler's book and argued that the law in Galatians was indeed the Ten Commandments. To be fair, both sides thought they were contending for truth against heresy. Both sides believed God was leading them. Both sides thought their motives were pure. As this intense doctrinal division was growing in the field, and as the Minneapolis conference loomed on the horizon, the little lady who knew Jesus so well had some very important things to say *to both sides.*

Along with many others, Ellen White saw the growing movement for the enforcement of Sunday laws in America. She knew that this was no time for Adventist leaders to be divided. With deep spiritual perception, she discerned the subtle peril of self-righteousness popping up in Battle Creek *and* in California. So, on February 18, 1887, in the same month Waggoner's book was published, she fired off a letter to both Jones and Waggoner entitled, "Cautions About Making Doctrinal Differences Prominent; Contemplating The Marvels and Mysteries of the Incarnation." This is the letter I have come to call, "The Forgotten Manuscript That Shaped Minneapolis." A copy was sent to Elder Butler and to Uriah Smith, editor of *The Review and Herald,* so that they too might profit from the counsel. This manuscript is highly relevant for us today, especially in the light of ongoing conflicts within Adventism between some who consider themselves God-led reformers with a special message for the Church and some of the "conference brethren."

To the youthful *Signs* editors came this unexpected rebuke, which fell like lightning from a clear blue sky:

> If you, my brethren, had the experience that my husband and my-self have had in regard to these known differences being published in articles in our papers, you would never have pursued the course you have, either in your ideas advanced before our students and the college, neither would it have appeared in *Signs.* Especially at this time should everything like differences be repressed. These young men [Jones and Waggoner] are more self-confident and less cautious than they should be. . . . Even if you are fully convinced that your ideas of doctrine are sound, you do not show wisdom that these differences should be made apparent.
>
> I have no hesitancy in saying you have made a mistake here. You have departed from the positive directions God has given upon this matter, and only harm will result. This is not in God's order. You have now set the example for others to do as you have done, to feel at liberty to put in their various ideas and theories and bring them before the public, because you have done this. This will bring in a state of things you do not dream of. . . .
>
> It is no small matter for you to come out in *Signs* as you have done, and God has plainly revealed that such things should not be done. We must keep before the world a united front. Satan will triumph to see differences among Seventh-day Adventists. . . . The Reformation was

greatly retarded by making prominent differences on some points of faith and each party holding tenaciously to those things where they differed. We shall see eye to eye erelong, but to become firm and consider it your duty to present your views in decided opposition to the faith or truth as it has been taught by us as a people, is a mistake, and will result in harm, and only harm, as in the days of Martin Luther. Begin to draw apart and feel at liberty to express your ideas without reference to the views of your brethren, and a state of things will be introduced that you do not dream of.

My husband had some ideas on some points differing from the views taken by his brethren. I was shown that however true his views were, God did not call for him to put them in front before his brethren and create differences of ideas. . . . There are the main pillars of our faith, subjects which are of vital interest, the Sabbath, the keeping of the commandments of God. . . . If these things come into our conference, I would refuse to attend one of them; for I have had so much light upon this subject that I know that unconsecrated and unsanctified hearts would enjoy this kind of exercise. . . . Nothing would suite them better than a sharp discussion. . . . Too late in the day, brethren, too late in the day.

We are in the great day of atonement, a time when a man must be afflicting his soul, confessing his sins, humbling his heart before God, and getting ready for the great conflict. When these contentions come in before the people, they will think one has the argument, and then that another directly opposed has the argument. The poor people will become confused. . . . There must be decided efforts to handle, to publish with pen and voice these things that will reveal only harmony.

Elder [J. H.] Waggoner [E. J. Waggoner's father] has loved discussions and contention. I fear that E. J. W. [the son] has cultivated a love for the same. We need now good, humble religion. E. J. W. needs humility, meekness, and Brother Jones can be a power for good if he will constantly cultivate practical godliness, that he may teach this to the people. . . . I am satisfied that we must have more of Jesus and less of self. If there is a difference upon any parts of understanding of some particular passage of Scripture, then do not be with pen or voice making your differences apparent and making a breach when there is no need of this.

We are one in faith in the fundamental truths of God's word. And one object must be kept in view constantly, that is harmony and cooperation must be maintained without compromising one principle of truth. . . . We have a worldwide message. The commandments of God and the testimonies of Jesus Christ are the burden of our work. To have unity and love for one another is the great work now to be carried on. . . . There has been a door thrown open for variance and strife and contention and differences which none of you can see but God. His eye traces the beginning to the end. And the magnitude of mischief God alone knows. The bitterness, the wrath, the resentment, the jealousies, the heart burnings provoked by controversies of both sides of the question causes the loss of many souls. . . .

There is to be closed every door that will lead to points of difference and debate among brethren. . . . There is altogether too little of the love of Christ in the hearts of those who claim to believe the truth. While all their hopes are centered in Jesus Christ, while His Spirit pervades the soul, then there will be unity, although every idea may not be exactly the same on all points. . . . Man has to learn himself before God can do great things with him. . . . Altogether too little meekness and humility are brought into the work of searching for the truth as for hidden treasures, and if the truth were taught in Jesus, there would be a hundredfold greater power, and it would be a converting power upon human hearts, but everything is so mingled with self that the wisdom from above cannot be imparted.[2]

As a lowly bush burned brightly in the Sinai desert, so should the following twelve penetrating facts from this "Forgotten Manuscript" burn deeply into our souls:

1. "We have a worldwide message."
2. "We must keep before the world a united front."
3. God has given "positive direction" that all "differences should be repressed."
4. "However true" our ideas may be, if they are not part of "the pillars," and if they create division, we should not push them to the front.
5. The *Signs* articles penned by Jones and Waggoner were "a mistake" even though they considered it their conscientious "duty" to publish them.
6. "Self-confidence" and a lack of "caution" had been exhibited.
7. The *Signs* articles set "an example" for others "to draw apart and feel at liberty to express [their] ideas without reference to the views of [their] brethren."
8. A "condition of things" would result which they did not dream of.
9. Our own people would become "confused."
10. This would "cause the loss of many souls."

11. There is need for greater "humility," "meekness," "cooperation," and "harmony" in order "to have unity and love for one another" which is "the great work now to be carried on."

12. If "the truth were taught in Jesus" there would be "a hundredfold greater power" than is now revealed in the preaching of the third angel's message.

When E. J. Waggoner received this testimony and read it carefully, it pierced his soul. Because his heart was open to being corrected by His Lord, he realized that the True Witness was speaking directly to him. Try to picture him pondering these sentences: "You have made a mistake here . . . only harm will result." "These young men are more self-confident and less cautious than they should be." "E. J. W. needs humility." "Man has to learn himself before God can do great things through him."

Alone in his Pacific Press® office, Ellet J. Waggoner searched his heart, struggled with self, and prayed.

By the grace of God, he gained the victory.

On April 1, 1887, from Oakland, California, Waggoner wrote this response to Ellen White. His words are worthy of careful study.

Dear Sister White,

It is several days since Brother Jones sent me the testimony which you so kindly sent to us. I wish to thank you for it, and to express my gratitude to God that His Spirit still strives with me, pointing out the errors to which I am so subject. I have read the Testimony several times very carefully, and the more I read it, the more convinced I am that it was timely and was needed. I have been able to see some things in my heart of which I was unconscious. I thought I was actuated by nothing but pure motives and love for the truth, in what I have said and written, but I can see plainly that there has been very much love of self mixed in.

I can see how I have really hindered the advancement of the truth, when I thought I was helping it. That testimony has been blessed by the Lord to my good.

I have been looking at myself in the light of the word of God, and have been conscious of my insignificance as never before. As I have humbled myself before God, He has heard my prayer, and has given me a measure of peace greater than I have known before. Again I thank God for the Testimony of His Spirit. The strongest proof to me of their genuineness is that they have revealed to me my heart to an extent that it could not possibly be known by any one beside God.

I have nothing to say in self-justification. . . . As you say, I have been confident that I was correct; my error has been in being too hasty in putting forth views which could arouse controversy. I think I have learned a lesson that I shall not forget. I hope and pray that I may not. I do desire most earnestly that the time may soon come when all our people shall see eye to eye. In my unconscious self-sufficiency, I supposed that I could do much toward accomplishing this. I have learned that God will accomplish His work in His own way, and that the strongest efforts in the best cause are powerless when not prompted solely by love to God, and accompanied by a total hiding of self in Christ. Oh, I do want the righteousness of Christ; I want to have communion with Him, and continually know the love that passeth knowledge.

I can see that I have allowed a spirit of controversy to creep in altogether too much. I have been to a certain extent conscious of this, and have striven against it. I have not desired it; but I have not been satisfied with myself. I can say that as I have been able to see more of the loveliness of the character of Christ, in contrast with myself, I am heartily sick of all strife. I am determined, by the help of the Lord, that my writings shall be characterized by more of the love of God. I do pray that this reproof from the Lord may indeed continue to work in me the peaceable fruits of righteousness. I can say of a truth, that I do not cherish the slightest feeling of anything like ill feeling toward any of my brethren. I am truly sorry for the feeling that has existed and does exist between the two offices [Pacific Press® and Review®]. . . .

I know full well that a feeling of criticism has been allowed to creep in here, and I think in no one more than me. As I now view the spirit of criticism, which springs from the meanest kind of pride, I hate it, and want no more of it. I am determined that henceforth no word of mine, either in public or in private, shall tend to the detraction of any worker in the cause of God. I do want to abide in Christ, and to have His Spirit dwelling in me, so that the love of Christ, and that alone may constrain me in all that I do, and that all that I do may have the divine impress.

I do want to be in that condition of daily growth in grace, that while I remain connected with *Signs* it may carry with it only the atmosphere of heaven and may contain nothing that will repel an honest seeker after truth, or offend a humble child of God. Oh, for the wisdom that comes from above! Will you pray for me? Thanking you again for your kind admonition, I remain, your brother, in hope of eternal life,

E. J. Waggoner[3]

When Waggoner stepped off the train at Minneapolis, he walked with humble steps. No longer did he feel superior to his "conference brethren." As a duly appointed delegate to the 1888 General Conference Session, he considered it an inestimable privilege to share the good news of the righteousness of Jesus Christ with his fellow workers. Feeling his own weakness and his need for a Savior, *he was now a messenger prepared to give a message.*

When the time came for him to step onto the platform to begin his devotional lectures, he was fully aware that "a servant of the Lord must not quarrel but be gentle to all, able to teach, patient" (2 Timothy 2:24). After bowing his head for prayer with his fellow delegates, the promise of Jesus was fulfilled, "It is not you who speak, but the Spirit of your Father who speaks in you" (Matthew 10:20). After watching closely how God's messenger conducted himself while communicating His message, Ellen White later wrote, "Elder Waggoner had taken a straightforward course, not involving personalities, to thrust anyone or to ridicule anyone. He conducted the subject as a Christian gentleman should, in a kind and courteous manner."[4]

To his credit, Elder Jones also responded positively to the February 1887 rebuke. On March 13, 1887, from Healdsburg, California, he penned this response to Ellen White.

> Dear Sister White,
> Your letter to myself and Bro. E. J. Waggoner reached me three days ago. I have read it carefully three or four times, and have now sent it to him. For my part I thank the Lord for His goodness in showing me where I have done wrong, and shall try earnestly to profit by the testimony. I am sorry indeed that I have had any part in anything that would tend to create division or do any harm to the cause of God. And I shall be particularly guarded in the future. . . . Again thanking you for your kind admonition, and promising to follow it closely in the future, and endeavor to redeem the past, I remain, very respectfully, your obedient servant,
> Alonzo T. Jones[5]

At the 1893 General Conference, A. T. Jones was also a messenger prepared to give a message. Although armed with solid Bible truth, the spirit he manifested in 1893 was similar to what his friend, E. J. Waggoner, had revealed five years earlier at Minneapolis. Speaking to his fellow General Conference delegates about the Laodicean message, Jones said humbly,

> I ask you, now to start with, do not place me up here as one who is separated from you, and above you, and as talking down to you, and excluding myself from the things that may be presented. I am with you in all these things. I, with you, just as certainly, and just as much, need

to be prepared to receive what God has to give us, as anybody else on earth. So I beg of you not to separate me from you in this matter. . . . What I want, brethren, is simply to seek God with you, with all the heart, [Congregation—"Amen"] and to have everything out of the way, that God may give us what He has for us.[6]

These enlightening testimonies are extremely relevant to us today as we stand on the brink of the final events that will soon burst upon the world with blinding speed. We must not only understand the message, but we must also be messengers prepared to give that message. That February 18, 1887, letter is for us. *It is for you.* Jesus said to Peter, "Satan has asked for you. . . . But I have prayed for you. . . . When you have returned to Me [been converted], strengthen your brethren" (Luke 22:31, 32).

Do we need to be converted?

Before his conversion, John Wesley moaned, "I went to America to convert the Indians, but, oh, who shall convert me?"[7] The answer is: only Jesus Christ. When we are truly converted, we also will seek unity, not involve personalities, and conduct ourselves as proper Christian gentlemen and women. In God's mysterious providence, that old and dusty "Forgotten Manuscript That Shaped Minneapolis" speaks to us today. It reveals that only humble messengers who love their brethren will receive "a hundredfold greater power" to proclaim the third angel's message at the close of time.

Will *you* be one of those messengers?

Will I?

May God help us.

---

1. See *The National Sunday Law: Arguments of Alonzo T. Jones before the United States Senate Committee on Education and Labor on Dec. 13, 1888.* Available from Laymen Ministries, 1-800-245-1844.

2. *1888 Materials,* 21–31.

3. *Manuscripts and Memories of Minneapolis* (Nampa, ID: Pacific Press®, 1988), 71, 72.

4. Manuscript 24, 1888.

5. *Manuscripts and Memories of Minneapolis,* 66, 67.

6. *1893 General Conference Bulletin,* 164, 165.

7. Albert C. Outler, ed., *John Wesley* (New York: Oxford University Press, 1964), 44.

CHAPTER TWENTY-ONE

ARE YOU READY FOR THE RAIN?

"FIRE CONDITIONS ARE GETTING WORSE EVERY DAY THAT WE HAVE
NO RAIN."
—Ben Wolcott, deputy chief of field operations, Florida Division of Forestry

The word of God predicts, "He [God] will come to us like the rain, like the latter and former rain to the earth" (Hosea 6:3). Here the personal presence of Jesus is compared to rain, and in the Bible the latter rain represents the final coming of the Holy Spirit to His people right before the end. The Scripture also proclaims,

> Be glad then, you children of Zion, and rejoice in the Lord your God; for He has given you the former rain faithfully, and He will cause the rain to come down for you—the former rain, and the latter rain in the first month (Joel 2:23).

In the margin of this text in the King James Version, the expression "former rain" is translated, "teacher of righteousness." Thus the former rain, which occurred at Pentecost, and the latter rain, which occurs right before Jesus returns, represents the coming of the Holy Spirit as a teacher of righteousness. Isaiah also compared the Holy Spirit to rain. "For I will pour water on him who is thirsty, and floods on the dry ground; I will pour My Spirit on your descendants, and My blessing on your offspring" (Isaiah 44:3). The prophet connected the descent of the Holy Spirit with righteousness and salvation from sin. "Rain down, you heavens, from above, and let the skies pour down righteousness; let the earth open, let them bring forth salvation, and let righteousness spring up together" (Isaiah 45:8). Notice this special statement written for

God's people two years after the Minneapolis conference: "God designs that the plan of salvation shall come to His people as the latter rain."[1]

Thus it is a fuller understanding of the plan of salvation—which is at the heart of the third angel's message—that is to come to us "as the latter rain." Isaiah wrote that when this occurs, "righteousness" will "spring up." How will this happen? Here's the answer: "When, as erring, sinful beings, we come to Christ and become partakers of His pardoning grace, love springs up in the heart."[2] This unselfish love, which is real righteousness, will spring up in our hearts when we fully receive the message of the imputed righteousness of Jesus Christ, without works, and the gift of the Holy Spirit as a Teacher of Righteousness.

" 'This is the heritage of the servants of the Lord, and their righteousness is from Me,' says the LORD" (Isaiah 54:17).

Notice this amazing dialog between A. T. Jones and his fellow delegates at the 1893 General Conference Session:

> I received a letter a little while ago from Brother Starr in Australia, I will read two or three sentences because they come in well just at this place in our lessons:—Sister White says that we have been in the time of the latter rain since the Minneapolis meeting.[3]

> What is the loud cry? [Congregation: "The message of the righteousness of Christ."] "The loud cry has already begun in the message of the righteousness of Christ." Where does the latter rain come from? [Congregation: "From God."] All of it? [Congregation: "Yes."] What is it? "The Spirit of God." Now let us just put two things together. The teaching of righteousness according to righteousness—the message of righteousness—that is the loud cry; that is the latter rain; that is the righteousness of Christ. . . .

> The latter rain comes down from heaven. How much of the latter rain comes out of me? [Congregation: "None of it."] How much of it can I manufacture? [Congregation: "Not any."] . . . Where does it come from? [Congregation: "Heaven."] Will you take it that way? . . . Is there anybody in this house tonight willing and ready to take righteousness from heaven? [Congregation: "Amen!"] . . . Whoever is willing to take righteousness from heaven can receive the latter rain [Congregation: "Amen!"]; whoever is not, but wants the Lord to get some of it out of him, he cannot have the latter rain, he cannot have the righteousness of God, he cannot have the message of the righteousness of Christ.[4]

> When that message of God's righteousness—the righteousness of God which is by faith of Jesus Christ . . . when that is received and is

allowed to be carried on, and is held by His people . . . it will be but a short time until the whole thing is done. . . . Now is the time that the work will be closed up shortly, and we are in the midst of the scenes that close up this world's history. . . . We have been praying for the latter rain here at this Conference already, haven't we? . . . I simply ask you now, are you ready to receive the latter rain?[5]

Were they ready? During the years that followed 1888 and 1893, Satan continued to work beneath the surface to nourish subtle "roots of self" and feelings of bitterness between brethren. As a result, Ellen White's solemn appeal for unity in Jesus and in the message of Christ's righteousness went unheeded by many. Thirteen years passed after Minneapolis, and the latter rain had not come. Then came the General Conference Session of 1901. This was the last session ever held in Battle Creek. All heaven hoped that there the latter rain could finally be poured out. Yet, in spite of the many good things that occurred at that conference, the full desire of Jesus Christ was not realized.

In January of 1903, in California, Ellen White was reflecting and writing about "the work that might have been done at the last [1901] General Conference."[6] As her pen moved back and forth, she suddenly "lost consciousness" and "seemed to be witnessing a scene in Battle Creek," at the very place where the 1901 Conference had been held two years earlier. Notice carefully:

We were assembled in the auditorium of the Tabernacle. Prayer was offered, a hymn was sung, and prayer was again offered. Most earnest supplication was made to God. The meeting was marked by the presence of the Holy Spirit. The work went deep, and some present were weeping aloud.

One arose from his bowed position and said that in the past he had not been in union with certain ones and had felt no love for them, but that now he saw himself as he was. With great solemnity he repeated the message to the Laodicean church: "Because thou sayest, I am rich, and increased with goods, and have need of nothing. In my self-sufficiency this is just the way I felt," he said. " 'And knowest not that thou art wretched, and miserable, and poor, and blind, and naked.' I now see that this is my condition. My eyes are opened. My spirit has been hard and unjust. I thought myself righteous, but my heart is broken, and I see my need of the precious counsel of the One who has searched me through and through. Oh, how gracious and compassionate and loving are the words, 'I counsel thee to buy of Me gold tried in the fire, that thou mayest be rich; and white raiment, that thou mayest be clothed, and that the shame of thy nakedness do not appear; and anoint thine eyes with eyesalve, that thou mayest see' " (Revelation 3:17, 18).

The speaker turned to those who had been praying, and said: "We have something to do. We must confess our sins, and humble our hearts before God." He made heartbroken confessions and then stepped up to several of the brethren, one after another, and extended his hand, asking forgiveness. Those to whom he spoke sprang to their feet, making confession and asking forgiveness, and they fell upon one another's necks, weeping. The spirit of confession spread through the entire congregation. It was a Pentecostal season. God's praises were sung, and far into the night, until early morning, the work was carried on.

The following words were often repeated, with clear distinctiveness: "As many as I love, I rebuke and chasten: be zealous therefore, and repent. Behold, I stand at the door and knock: if any man hear My voice, and open the door, I will come in to him, and sup with him, and he with Me" (Verses 19, 20). No one seemed to be too proud to make heartfelt confession, and those who led in this work were the ones who had influence, but had not before had courage to confess their sins. There was rejoicing such as never before had been heard in the Tabernacle.

Then I aroused from my unconsciousness, and for a while could not think where I was. My pen was still in my hand. The words were spoken to me: "This might have been. All this the Lord was waiting to do for His people. All heaven was waiting to be gracious." I thought of where we might have been had thorough work been done at the last General Conference [1901], and an agony of disappointment came over me as I realized that what I had witnessed was not a reality.[7]

Dear reader, "What might have been" must happen. In the first century, "When the Day of Pentecost had fully come, they were all with one accord in one place" (Acts 2:1). Peter had confessed to John, and James had made everything right with Andrew. They were united in the message and in the experience of Christ our Righteousness. This is our work too. And those who have influence should lead out. Let's be among those who "see so much work to do, so many fellow beings to help, that they will have no time to look for faults in others. They will have no time to work on the negative side."[8] It is a frightening fact that "many become absorbed in looking and listening for evil" and "forget what a great sin they are committing."[9]

A ship sailing the high seas ran into an awful storm and began to sink. The lifeboat was big enough to hold most of the passengers, but not all. One poor man clung to the side of the boat and struggled to climb in. Those inside were so fearful that his extra weight would sink them all that one man took a knife and cut off the struggler's hand. In desperation, the dying man promptly held on with his other hand. Without mercy, his other hand was sliced off too. Staring death in the face, the poor soul finally grasped the side of the boat with his teeth! Moved with compassion, the people inside the boat at last decided to pull the man aboard. But oh, how much better if they had done so before cutting off his hands!

Dear friend, a horrific storm is soon to burst upon the world and the church, and sadly, the majority will sink beneath the waves. Demonic sharks lurk throughout these waters, and some people are even now just barely holding on with their teeth. Shall we not have compassion on each other and do all we can to lift the erring into the boat? Instead of cutting off each other's hands, let's pray for each other and overcome our own tendency to use the knife. This is one of the "great sins" that we must overcome in order to receive the latter rain. It is also a sure symptom of self-righteousness. As it is written, "He spoke this parable to some who trusted in themselves that they were righteous, and despised others" (Luke 18:9). Listen, "It is left with us to remedy the defects in our characters, to cleanse the soul temple of every defilement. Then the latter rain will fall upon us as the early rain fell upon the disciples on the day of Pentecost."[10]

"Suddenly there came a sound from heaven, as of a rushing mighty wind, and it filled the whole house where they were sitting. . . . And they were all filled with the Holy Spirit" (Acts 2:2, 4). On the day of Pentecost,

> the revelation of Christ by the Holy Spirit brought to them a realizing sense of His power and majesty, and they stretched forth their hands unto Him by faith, saying, "I believe" [righteousness by faith]. Thus it was in the time of the early rain; but the latter rain will be more abundant. The Savior of men will be glorified, and the earth will be lightened with the bright shining of the beams of His righteousness.[11]

"Ask the Lord for rain," wrote the ancient prophet, "in the time of the latter rain. The Lord will make flashing clouds; He will give them showers of rain" (Zechariah 10:1). "He will come to us like the rain" (Hosea 6:3). The promise is sure. The Great Day is coming. I appeal to all who read this book, let's put away our differences and unite on the platform of Jesus Christ and His righteousness. Storm clouds are gathering. Can't you hear the muffled sounds of thunder in the distance? It is the sound of rain. " 'A shower is coming,' " Jesus says. "How is it you do not discern this time?" (Luke 12:54, 56).

I ask you the same question that A. T. Jones asked his brethren in 1893, "Are *you* ready to receive the latter rain?"

I hope so.

Here is Heaven's prophecy of the future:

"Clad in the armor of Christ's righteousness, the church is to enter upon her final conflict."[12]

---

1. *1888 Materials,* 1690.
2. White, *Steps to Christ,* 59.
3. *1893 General Conference Bulletin,* 377.
4. Ibid., 359.
5. Ibid., 243.
6. White, *Testimonies,* 8:104.
7. Ibid., 104–106.
8. Ibid., 83.
9. Ibid.
10. Ibid., 5:214.
11. *The Review and Herald,* November 29, 1892.
12. White, *Prophets and Kings,* 725.

CHAPTER TWENTY-TWO

WHEN THE BOMB DROPS

"THE DARKER THE NIGHT, THE BRIGHTER THE STARS."
—Friedrich Schlotterbeck (1909–1979),
German author and anti-Nazi resistance leader

On December 7, 1941, Japanese warplanes approached the island of Oahu in the Pacific. Their destination: Pearl Harbor. About 8:00 A.M., thousands of bombs began dropping from the skies upon an unprepared United States naval base. When the surprise attack ended, 2,403 people had been ushered into eternity, with another 1,139 wounded. The tragedy of that fateful day launched America into World War II. The battle cry was raised, "Remember Pearl Harbor."

Another surprise attack lies just around the corner. For two thousand years, Satan has been preparing for it. From the arsenal of hell, "the mark of the beast" will drop unexpectedly upon the inhabitants of this world, and the majority will be bombed out of eternal life. "He causes all, both small and great, rich and poor, free and slave, to receive a mark on their right hand or on their foreheads" (Revelation 13:16). Jesus called this final period of earth's history "the hour of trial which shall come upon the whole world, to test those who dwell on the earth" (Revelation 3:10).

The "spirit of prophecy" (see Revelation 12:17; 19:10), manifested through the writings of Ellen White, has sounded the warning that many—even among Seventh-day Adventists who should know better—will be caught off guard when the enemy strikes.

The time is not far distant when the test will come to every soul. The mark of the beast will be urged upon us. Those who have step by step yielded to worldly demands and conformed to worldly customs will not find it a hard matter to yield to the powers that be, rather than to subject themselves to derision, insult, threatened imprisonment, and death. The contest is between the commandments of God and the commandments of men. In this time the gold will be separated from the dross in the church. True godliness will be clearly distinguished from the appearance and tinsel of it. Many a star that we have admired for its brilliancy will then go out in darkness. Chaff like a cloud will be borne away on the wind, even from places where we see only floors of rich wheat. All who assume the ornaments of the sanctuary, but are not clothed with Christ's righteousness, will appear in the shame of their own nakedness.[1]

The Bible predicts that in the closing moments of time, the mark of the beast will be enforced by earthly governments in response to a global crisis. Devastating earthquakes, hurricanes, fires, floods, fear, confusion, economic meltdowns, bankruptcy, violence, and gross immorality will eventually become so unbearable that world religions and governments will at last unite in a desperate attempt to force humanity to do what seems reasonable: return to God. During World War II, Americans cried, "Remember Pearl Harbor." Thirty-four hundred years ago the Almighty thundered from His mountain pulpit, "Remember the Sabbath day to keep it holy" (Exodus 20:8). During earth's final crisis, governments around the globe will yield to religious pressure to enforce—in a misguided effort to bring our world closer to God—a Roman Catholic tradition that states, "Remember Sunday to keep it holy."[2]

The Seventh-day Adventist interpretation of Bible prophecy—which I believe to be correct—is that when Sunday laws are finally legislated worldwide, this will constitute enforcement on a global scale of a "mark" of papal Rome's illegitimate authority—"the mark of the beast."[3]

If you are not a Seventh-day Adventist and find such a scenario hard to fathom, consider carefully what happened right after September 11, 2001, when New York City's Twin Towers came crashing down. That day fell on a Tuesday. Three days later, on Friday, key representatives of the world's largest religions—Muslim, Catholic, Protestant, Jewish—met together for a special church service for prayer and to promote unity, inside the Washington National Cathedral in Washington D.C. Two days later, on Sunday, September 16, church attendance went through the roof around the world.

Don't miss this point.

More people attended church on the Sunday following September 11, 2001 than ever before.

Now think about it. On Tuesday, the crisis hit. Friday witnessed a move

WHEN THE BOMB DROPS | 145

for unity, and on Sunday millions all over planet Earth flocked to church. The sequence was: crisis, unity, Sunday. Get it? Make no mistake about it. When earth's last great crisis hits, the same sequence will be repeated. World religions and the general public will once again rush to church *on Sunday* to seek God and to ask Him to heal the planet of a seemingly insolvable mess.

When the crisis deepens, and when things get really crazy, Sunday attendance will finally shift to Sunday legislation as world governments and religions unite in an attempt to force people to attend church and to pray.

For solid biblical evidence that this will indeed occur, read the book, *The Great Controversy,* by Ellen White, and the pocketbook, *Decoding the Mark of the Beast,* available from White Horse Media.

When that fearful time finally arrives, the living issue will be: whom will we choose? The beast or the Lamb? What day will we keep? The true Bible Sabbath, "the seventh day" (Exodus 20:10), or Sunday, "the first day of the week" (Mark 16:2), which history informs us replaced God's Sabbath through the will of the Roman Catholic Church.

In the final analysis, the mysterious mark of the beast is simply the enforcement on a global scale of a specific sin of breaking one of the Ten Commandments at the end of time (see Daniel 7:25; Revelation 13:16, 17; 14:9–12). When the crisis comes, the Maker of heaven and earth will meet the issue by giving the special power of the latter rain (see Revelation 18:1) to a faithful remnant (see Revelation 12:17) that will boldly proclaim the third angel's message with a loud voice:

> Then a third angel followed them, saying with a loud voice, "If anyone worships the beast and his image, and receives his mark on his forehead or on his hand, he himself shall also drink of the wine of the wrath of God, which is poured out full strength into the cup of His indignation. He shall be tormented with fire and brimstone in the presence of the holy angels and in the presence of the Lamb. And the smoke of their torment ascends forever and ever; and they have no rest day or night, who worship the beast and his image, and whoever receives the mark of his name" (Revelation 14:9–12).

This final message will not be preached to the world from the writings of Jones and Waggoner. Neither will it be preached primarily from the writings of Ellen White, although the worldwide distribution of her books (such as *The Great Controversy*) will have an influence. Nor will it be called "The 1888 Message." Definitely not. Instead, it will be called what Jesus Christ Himself in the book of Revelation has named it.

The third angel's message.

And it will be preached from the Bible.

Who will preach it at the end? Based on what you have discovered in this book, you now know that it will be a united network of humble people who not only understand the message but who have also been prepared by the Lord to give that message. Having first experienced the Laodicean message, which the True Witness has given to them, they will be able to give the third angel's message to the world. In humility, love, and pitying tenderness toward those in the greatest danger of permanently receiving the deadly mark of sin upon their characters, they will lift up the Ten Commandments and the gospel of Jesus Christ.

As the remnant reveal the true character of God and exalt His true law of righteousness, this will expose the mark of the beast and the absence of righteousness in its advocates. During that crisis hour, the Holy Spirit will convict sinners like never before that they are indeed guilty lawbreakers before God (see Romans 3:19). Then Jesus Christ and His righteousness alone will be exalted as the only hope for a doomed world. With deep feeling, the Crucified One will be presented, and sinners will behold "the Lamb of God who takes away the sin of the world!" (John 1:29). On Calvary, Jesus died for every sin, including the sin of Sabbath-breaking. Those who don't resist His great love will forsake their sins and in utter helplessness cast themselves upon the merits of a crucified and risen Savior. The Father will say about every soul who does this, "Bring out the best robe and put it on him" (Luke 15:22). Through child-like faith in His blood, every repentant soul will receive complete remission of "sins that were previously committed" (Romans 3:25) and will be clothed with the spotless garment of the righteousness of Jesus Christ (see Isaiah 61:10).

"Much more then," penned Paul, will those newly "justified by His blood . . . be saved from wrath through Him" (Romans 5:9). During the final crisis, this wrath will be "the wine of the wrath of God" warned about in the third angel's message, which will be poured out in the seven last plagues on all who receive the mark of the beast (see Revelation 14:9–11; 16:1, 2). The only way to avoid this wrath is through repentance and faith in Jesus' blood (see Acts 20:21; Romans 3:25). Thus those who are justified by His blood will be protected from the judgments that Bible prophecy plainly predicts will fall on all who willingly continue to violate God's Law. This is how justification by faith is "the third angel's message in verity."[4]

As multitudes respond to Jesus' tender love during the final crisis and surrender their lives wholly to Him, Christ will come into their hearts, bringing His righteousness with Him. Through the gift of the special power of the Holy Spirit that brings the love of God into their hearts, these saints will be supernaturally enabled to "keep the commandments of God and the faith of Jesus" (Revelation 14:12). Thus they will join the "remnant of her seed, who keep the commandments of God and have the testimony of Jesus Christ" (Revelation 12:17, KJV). When everyone has made his or her final choice, Jesus will then close human probation with this solemn announcement: "He who is unjust, let him be unjust still; he who is filthy, let him be filthy still; he who is righteous, let him be righteous still; he who is holy, let him be holy still" (Revelation 22:11).

Thus the final saints will not only be counted righteous through the imputed righteousness of Christ, but they will also "be righteous still" through faith in Christ, by the power of the indwelling Spirit of God. Fully clothed in white robes, they will be prepared for the return of King Jesus on a white cloud. "I looked, and behold, a white cloud, and on the cloud sat One like the Son of Man, having on His head a golden crown, and in His hand a sharp sickle" (Revelation 14:14).

After being airlifted off planet Earth alive at the Second Coming, God's saints will be happily transported beyond the stars to the New Jerusalem. Before entering its pearly gates, this final benediction will be spoken by the One who died for them in A.D. 31 and who saved them by His marvelous grace. "Blessed are those who do His commandments, that they may have the right to the tree of life, and may enter through the gates into the city" (Revelation 22:14).

What a day that will be when the saints go marching in! The following summary puts the pieces together:

> The Lord God of heaven will not send upon the world His judgments for disobedience and transgression until He has sent His watchmen to give the warning. He will not close up the period of probation until the message shall be more distinctly proclaimed.
> The law of God is to be magnified; its claims must be presented in their true, sacred character, that the people may be brought to decide for or against the truth. Yet the work will be cut short in righteousness. The message of Christ's righteousness is to sound from one end of the earth to the other to prepare the way of the Lord. This is the glory of God, which closes the work of the third angel.[5]

One of the strangest events in all of military history took place when the Allies were about to invade Normandy in 1944. Field Marshal Erwin Rommel, called the Desert Fox, was in charge of Hitler's forces in northern France. On June 4, two days before the invasion, Rommel took a temporary leave of absence and returned to Germany. Why? Two reasons. First, he was informed by the German navy that storms and high seas in the English Channel would prohibit an Allied invasion. Second, June 6 was his wife's birthday.

On the morning of June 6 Rommel received word that the landing had taken place. It was too late. It was the beginning of the end. The "Fox" is said to have replied, "How stupid of me."

Soon there was no more Third Reich.

At this very moment, the Father, His Son, and the Holy Spirit are preparing for a final landing and invasion of Satan's global empire. Are *we* ready? The latter rain is soon to fall, and the message of the righteousness of Jesus Christ is to circle the earth. "He will finish the work and cut it short *in righteousness*" (Romans 9:28). Are we prepared? We cannot afford to miss the message and end up on the side of the enemy. If we do, we will cry out in anguish with billions of lost souls at the end of the Millennium, *"How stupid of me!"* (see Revelation 20:11–13). Oh, may God help us to understand, experience, and proclaim with a loud voice "the grand test that is to decide the eternal destiny of a world—the commandments of God and the faith of Jesus."[6]

If we don't, who will?

During World War II, a Lutheran pastor named Martin Niemoller, imprisoned by the Nazis, wrote these famous words:

> When the Nazis came for the communists,
> I remained silent;
> I was not a communist.
>
> When they locked up the social democrats,
> I remained silent;
> I was not a social democrat.
>
> When they came for the trade unionists,
> I did not speak out;
> I was not a trade unionist.
>
> When they came for the Jews,
> I remained silent;
> I wasn't a Jew.
>
> When they came for me,
> there was no one left to speak out.
>
> Dear friend, soon it will be too late to say anything.

It is almost midnight. Heaven's odometer is about to click over to these three words, "It is done" (Revelation 16:17).

The time of test is just upon us, for the loud cry of the third angel has already begun in the revelation of the righteousness of Christ, the sin-pardoning Redeemer. This is the beginning of the light of the angel whose glory shall fill the whole earth.[7]

Soon this prediction will be fulfilled: "One interest will prevail, one subject will swallow up every other,—*Christ our Righteousness.*"[8]

God has spoken. Have you heard His voice? I hope and pray so. Soon planet Earth's last crisis will strike. Now is the time to understand the message and to receive a preparation to give that message. Now is the time to proclaim the third angel's message with a loud voice, centered in Jesus Christ our Righteousness, by the power of the Holy Spirit. May God unite our hearts in one accord, and may He strengthen us to share from the Bible the tender love of our Savior for a dying world.

---

1. White, *Testimonies,* 5:81.

2. For historical proof that the Roman Catholic Church changed the Sabbath into Sunday, see Appendix 4 and Steve Wohlberg's pocketbook, *Discovering the Lost Sabbath Truth,* available from White Horse Media.

3. For historical evidence that all major Protestants Reformers interpreted the beast to be the Roman Catholic Church, read Steve Wohlberg's book, *End Time Delusions,* available from White Horse Media. For a detailed biblical study about the mark of the beast, read Steve Wohlberg's pocketbook, *Decoding the Mark of the Beast,* available from White Horse Media.

4. White, *Selected Messages,* 1:372.

5. White, *Testimonies,* 6:19; emphasis added.

6. Manuscript 97, 1908.

7. *The Review and Herald,* November 22, 1892; emphasis added.

8. *The Review and Herald Extra,* December 23, 1890.

RECOMMENDED BOOKS BY A. T. JONES AND E. J. WAGGONER

If you wish to read some of the many books and pamphlets written by A. T. Jones and E. J. Waggoner during the Minneapolis era, Steve Wohlberg recommends:

Christ and His Righteousness, by E. J. Waggoner
The Gospel in Galatians, by E. J. Waggoner
Living By Faith, by E. J. Waggoner
Fathers of the Catholic Church, by E. J. Waggoner
Sunday: Origin of Its Observance in the Christian Church, by
    E. J. Waggoner
The Full Assurance of Faith, by E. J. Waggoner
The Power of Forgiveness, by E. J. Waggoner
Studies in the Book of Galatians, by A. T. Jones
1893 The Third Angel's Message (talks by A. T. Jones)
1895 The Third Angel's Message (talks by A. T. Jones)
The Consecrated Way, by A. T. Jones
The Empires of the Bible, by A. T. Jones
Great Empires of Bible Prophecy, by A. T. Jones
Ecclesiastical Empire, by A. T. Jones
The Two Republics, by A. T. Jones
The Spirit of the Papacy, by A. T. Jones
The Immaculate Conception, by A. T. Jones
Our God is a Consuming Fire, by A. T. Jones
Lessons on Faith, by Jones and Waggoner

Available from Laymen Ministries, 1-800-245-1844.

JESUS CHRIST,
LORD OF THE SABBATH DAY

S peaking to a group of hostile Pharisees, Jesus Christ boldly declared, "For the Son of Man is Lord even of *the Sabbath day*" (Matthew 12:8). By identifying Himself as the Lord of the Sabbath day, Jesus of Nazareth was revealing to His astonished hearers that He Himself, in cooperation with His Father, was the One who made planet Earth in six days and rested on the seventh day (see Genesis 1). Christ's statement to the Jews also reveals that He is "the Lord" specified in the fourth commandment (see Exodus 20:11).

The New Testament is clear that Jesus Christ is not only our Savior but also our Creator.

"All things were made through Him, and without Him nothing was made that was made" (John 1:3).

"He [Jesus] was in the world, and the world was made through Him, and the world did not know Him" (John 1:10).

"God . . . created all things through Jesus Christ" (Ephesians 3:9).

"For by Him [Jesus] all things were created that are in heaven and that are on earth, visible and invisible, whether thrones or dominions or principalities or powers. All things were created through Him and for Him" (Colossians 1:16).

Thus the One who created our world (Genesis 1), rested on the seventh day (Genesis 2:1–3), and wrote the fourth commandment on Mount Sinai (Exodus 20:8–11) with "the finger of God" (Exodus 31:18) is the same One who stretched out His hands and died on the cross for our sins (compare Exodus 3:14 with John 8:58 and 1 Corinthians 10:4 with 1 Corinthians 15:1–3).

What good news! Our Creator has become our Savior.

The seventh-day Sabbath reveals Jesus Christ as Lord of all.

THE FIRST DAY OF THE WEEK IN THE NEW TESTAMENT

The following is an examination of all eight New Testament verses mentioning the first day of the week, Sunday.

Matthew 28:1: "After the Sabbath, as the first day of the week began to dawn . . ." Here two different days are mentioned. One is the Sabbath, and the other is the first day of the week, or Sunday, which followed the Sabbath. Jesus Christ rose from the dead on Sunday, but Matthew says nothing about any switch from the Bible Sabbath to Sunday as a day of worship.

Mark 16:1, 2: "Now when the Sabbath was past, . . . very early in the morning, on the first day of the week . . ." The resurrection of Jesus on Sunday morning was glorious! Yet again, there is no evidence here that this made Sunday sacred. Did the cross make Friday sacred? As in Matthew 28:1, Sunday came "when the Sabbath was past," that is, the day after the Sabbath.

Mark 16:9: "[Jesus] rose early on the first day of the week." Sunday is simply called "the first day of the week." The first week began in Genesis. God made the world in six days, and then He "blessed the seventh day and sanctified it." He "rested on the seventh day" (Genesis 2:2, 3). God ordained "*the* seventh day" as His Holy Day (see Isaiah 58:13), not the first day of the week.

Luke 24:1: The women went to the tomb on the first day of the week after "they rested the Sabbath day according to the commandment" (Luke 23:56). This verse is enlightening. These were Christian women who loved Jesus and who kept the Sabbath *after Jesus died on the cross*. Luke was a Gentile who wrote this about twenty-eight years after the resurrection. As Luke states, the Sabbath was still there, and these Christian women were keeping it "according to the commandment" found in Exodus 20:8–11. This proves that the seventh-day Sabbath continued *after* the cross, and that the Sabbath is *not* Sunday.

John 20:1: Mary came to the tomb on "the first day of the week." As in Matthew, Mark, and Luke, John simply gives a narrative account of the resurrection of our Lord on Sunday.

John 20:19: "On the first day of the week" (late Sunday afternoon), the disciples "were assembled" behind shut doors. Why? "For fear of the Jews." This was not a worship service. They were scared. They had not believed reports from the women that Jesus had risen (see Mark 16:9–13). They were worried that the Jewish authorities might burst in, accuse them of stealing their Lord's body, and then arrest them. Then Jesus revealed Himself as the risen Lord. Yet in His post-resurrection appearances and teaching, He never mentioned Sunday.

1 Corinthians 16:2: "Concerning the collection for the saints" (verse 1). The context and other Scriptures reveal that Paul was raising a collection for needy believers in Jerusalem (verse 3) during a time of famine (see Acts 11:27–30; Romans 15:25, 26). Notice carefully: On "the first day of the week" (Sunday), "let each one of you" (individually) "lay something aside" (the original Greek word used here literally means, "at home"), "storing up" (placing in storage) a certain amount. The words "storing up" reveal that this was to be done by the believers *in their homes.* The "first day of the week" was ideal for the Corinthian believers to look back on the previous week, examine their finances, and set aside a weekly contribution. This would then be gathered and made ready for Paul, "that there be no gatherings when I come." Paul was going to pass through Corinth, and he wanted the money to be ready for him to pick up. Thus this was an emergency situation, and not their regular practice, for Paul had to give them orders to do what they were not normally used to doing (verse 1). *Here Paul said nothing about a Sunday church service or the resurrection.*

Acts 20:6–13: This passage is often used to support Sunday observance, but it doesn't. This was Paul's last meeting with a small group of believers in Troas (verse 6). The meeting took place at night (verses 7, 8) on the "first day of the week." Biblically, a new day begins at sunset (see Genesis 1:5, 8; Luke 23:54). *Therefore this meeting took place on a Saturday night.* The New English Bible translates Acts 20:7 as, "On Saturday night." That night Paul preached his farewell sermon, "ready to depart the next day [on Sunday morning]." At "daybreak" (verse 11), while Luke "sailed" (verse 15), Paul walked twenty-five miles "to Assos" (verse 14). *Thus Paul traveled many miles that Sunday.* He was in Troas for "seven days" (verse 6). Simple math reveals that Paul arrived on the previous Sunday, stayed for a week, and conducted his last meeting on Saturday night, right after the Sabbath. Significantly, the Book of Acts mentions "the first day of the week" only once (in Acts 20:7), yet the Sabbath is mentioned eleven times (see Acts 1:12; 13:14, 27, 42, 44; 15:21; 16:13; 17:2; 18:4). A careful study of Acts 20:6–13 reveals that the much-used "Saturday-Night-in-Troas-Sunday-Travel-to-Assos" text provides *convincing proof that Paul did not keep Sunday holy.*

SUMMARIZING THE NEW TESTAMENT EVIDENCE

Sunday is simply called, "the first day of the week" in the New Testament. Jesus Christ Himself never mentioned Sunday, *not even one time.*

Not once is Sunday set aside as a holy day in honor of the resurrection. In Matthew, Mark, and Luke, Sunday always comes *"after the Sabbath."*

The Holy Spirit only teaches what Jesus Christ taught (John 14:26; 16:13, 14). Because Jesus never mentioned Sunday, the Holy Spirit will not teach it.

After His resurrection, Jesus told His disciples to teach only what He had commanded them (see Matthew 28:20). Because Jesus never mentioned Sunday, the apostles could not have taught it.

Sunday cannot be part of the New Covenant because it began *after Jesus Christ's blood was shed.* After death, it is impossible to "add" to a covenant (see Galatians 3:15).

For more information about the Sabbath-versus-Sunday controversy, read Steve Wohlberg's pocketbook, *Discovering the Lost Sabbath Truth;* the book, *Sunday: The Origin of Its Observance in the Christian Church,* by E. J. Wagonner; or watch the fascinating five-part TV documentary, *The Seventh Day: Revelations from the Lost Pages of History,* produced by LLT Productions. Available from White Horse Media, 1-800-78-BIBLE.

HIDDEN HISTORY:
FROM SABBATH TO SUNDAY

The following is a historical survey of the change from Sabbath to Sunday, beginning with the entrance of sun worship into ancient Israel.

Sun worship infects ancient Israel: In the ancient world, sun worship was one of the most prevalent forms of pagan idolatry. Immediately after Israel left Egypt, God warned His people against being "driven to worship" the sun (Deuteronomy 4:19). Israel later yielded to temptation, compromised with the nations around them, and dedicated their "horses . . . to the sun" (2 Kings 23:11). During a time of revival, King Josiah purged much of Israel and "burned the chariots of the sun with fire" (2 Kings 23:11). Before the Babylonian captivity, many Israelite leaders rejected their Creator, yielded again to idolatry, and were "worshipping the sun toward the east" (Ezekiel 8:16). At the same time, God declared that they had "hidden their eyes from My Sabbaths" (Ezekiel 22:26). *Thus ancient Israel shifted from God's Sabbath to sun worship.* In 1 Corinthians 10:1–11, Paul warned the church against repeating ancient Israel's sins.

Sun worship, "the day of the sun," and "Sunday": The Romans called the sun god Mithra and Apollo, and they especially worshiped the sun on "the first day of the week," also called *dies Solis* (Latin), which means "day of the Sun." History reveals that the name Sunday was picked "because this day was anciently dedicated to the sun, or to its worship. The first day of the week."[1]

A predicted "falling away" within the church: Through the enlightenment of the Holy Spirit, Paul discerned that a tragic falling away from Jesus Christ and Bible truth would occur within Christianity and that "the man of sin" would arise (2 Thessalonians 2:3). This "man of sin" is the same power as the "little horn" with "eyes like the eyes of a man" (Daniel 7:8), and "the beast" (see Revelation 13). Even in his own day, Paul saw errors creeping into the church and declared, "The mystery of lawlessness is already at work" (2 Thessalonians 2:7). Paul warned that after his death, from among "the elders of the church" men would "rise up, speaking perverse things, to draw away the disciples after themselves" (Acts 20:17, 30). This apostasy would result in a departure from God's Word and the original faith as taught by Jesus Christ (see 1 Timothy 4:1). Other New Testament writers warned that deceptions were entering Christianity. See 2 Peter 2:1; 1 John 2:18, 19; Jude 3, 4.

Anti-Jewish sentiment fueled the Sabbath-to-Sunday shift: Near the end of His ministry, Jesus predicted that every stone of the Jewish temple would be "thrown down" (Matthew 24:1, 2). This occurred when, in A.D. 70, Romans destroyed the temple during the First Jewish War. When the Romans again made war with the Jews from 132–135, the Roman emperor Hadrian banished all Jews from Palestine. These Jewish wars took place *after* the book of Acts was written and resulted in great pressure upon the early Christian church to move away from anything that appeared Jewish, including the Sabbath. Because Sunday was already popular throughout the Roman Empire as a day for sun worship, some Christian leaders (often called the Early Church Fathers) yielded to temptation and began shifting from Sabbath to Sunday. "Jesus Christ rose on Sunday!" became their rationalizing cry. Thus they used the resurrection of our Lord, who "died for our sins" (1 Corinthians 15:3) of the breaking of God's Law (1 John 3:4), *as an excuse to break one of the Ten Commandments.*

Christians compromised with pagan sun worship practices and adopted Sunday as a day of rest:

> Before the coming of Christ, all the Eastern nations performed divine worship with their faces turned to that part of the heavens where the sun displays his rising beams . . . The Christian converts . . . retained the ancient and universal custom of worshiping toward the east, which sprang from it.[2]

"Sunday (Dies Solis, of the Roman calendar; 'day of the sun,' because it was dedicated to the sun), the first day of the week, was adopted by the early Christians as a day of worship."[3] "We all gather on the day of the sun . . . on this same day Jesus Christ our Savior rose from the dead."[4]

The Church in Rome becomes the Roman Catholic Church: Before the Jewish temple was destroyed in A.D. 70, a strong Christian church was planted through missionary efforts inside the city of Rome itself—in the heart of the Roman Empire. Paul wrote his letter, "The Epistle of Paul to the Romans," to "all who are in Rome, beloved of God, called to be saints" (Romans 1:7). But because it was surrounded by paganism inside the world's mightiest capital, the church in Rome soon experienced a "falling away" (2 Thessalonians 2:3) from the purity of the gospel and turned into the wealthy, politically savvy, powerful Roman Catholic Church. Much of this transition took place during the time of the Emperor Constantine (fourth century A.D.) who favored the Roman Church above all other Christian churches.

Constantine, sun worship, Catholicism, and Sunday: In A.D. 312, prior to his pivotal victory over his rival, Maxentius, at the Battle of the Milvian

Bridge, Constantine became a "Christian" after claiming to see in broad daylight a vision of "a cross above the sun" with these words emblazoned, *"in hoc signo vinces"* ("by this sign conquer"). After defeating his enemies and becoming Emperor of Rome, Constantine presided in full pomp over the First Council of Nicea in A.D. 325.

A shrewd political genius, his scheme was to unite paganism and Christianity to strengthen his disintegrating empire. Constantine knew that pagans throughout the empire worshiped the sun on the first day of the week, and he discovered that many Christians—especially in Rome and Alexandria—also kept Sunday because Christ rose from the dead on that day. So Constantine developed a plan to unite the groups on the common platform of Sunday-keeping. On March 7, 321, he passed his famous national Sunday law:

> Let all judges and townspeople and occupations of all trades rest on the venerable day of the Sun [Sunday]; nevertheless, let those who are situated in the rural districts freely and with full liberty attend to the cultivation of the fields, because it so frequently happens that no other day may be so fitting for ploughing grains or trenching vineyards, lest at the time the advantage of the moment granted by the provision of heaven may be lost.[5]

Now a professed Christian, Constantine nevertheless remained a devout sun worshipper. "The sun was universally celebrated as the invincible guide and protector of Constantine," notes Edward Gibbon in his classic *Decline and Fall of the Roman Empire.*[6] Constantine even printed coins that "bore on the one side the letters of the name of Christ, on the other the figure of the sun god."[7] Again, Constantine's promotion of Sunday observance was part of his strategy to combine paganism with Christianity:

The retention of the old pagan name of *dies Solis,* or "Sunday," for the weekly Christian festival, is *in great measure owing to the union of pagan and Christian sentiment* with which the first day of the week was recommended by Constantine to his subjects, pagan and Christian alike, as the "venerable day of the Sun."[8] "The Jewish, the Samaritan, even the Christian, were to be fused and recast into one great system, of which the sun was to be the central object of adoration."[9] In A.D. 330, Constantine moved his capital from Rome to Constantinople (modern Istanbul), thus preparing the way for the Roman Catholic popes to reign in Rome *as the successors of Constantine.* As papal Rome increased in power, it opposed Sabbath observance in favor of Sunday sacredness.

Many fifth-century Christians kept the Sabbath and Sunday: In spite of the rising popularity of Sunday sacredness, church historian Socrates

Scholasticus (fifth century) wrote: "For although almost all churches through-out the world celebrate the sacred mysteries [of the Lord's Supper] on the Sab-bath of every week, yet the Christians of Alexandria and at Rome, on account of some ancient tradition, have ceased to do this."[10] Another historian con-firmed this, stating, "The people of Constantinople, and almost everywhere, assemble together on the Sabbath, as well as on the first day of the week, which custom is never observed at Rome or at Alexandria."[11] Thus even in the fifth century, Sabbath-keeping was still prevalent (except in Rome and Alexandria), along with Sunday-keeping. Many Christians kept both days. But as the centu-ries wore on, Sunday-keeping grew in prominence, especially within Catholic territories. Today, the majority of Christians observe Sunday, but the question remains, *What does the Bible say?*

The Roman Catholic Church claims the change was her act:

"Question: Which is the Sabbath day?

"Answer: Saturday is the Sabbath day.

"Question: Why do we observe Sunday instead of Saturday?

"Answer: We observe Sunday instead of Saturday because the Cath-olic Church transferred the solemnity from Saturday to Sunday."[12]

But since Saturday, not Sunday, is specified in the Bible, isn't it curious that non-Catholics who profess to take their religion directly from the Bible and not from the Church, observe Sunday instead of Saturday? Yes, of course, it is inconsistent; but this change was made about fifteen centuries before Protestantism was born, and by that time the custom was universally observed. They have continued the custom, even though it rests upon the authority of the Catholic Church and not upon an explicit text in the Bible. The observance remains as a reminder of the Mother Church from which the non-Catholic sects broke away—like a boy running away from home but still carrying in his pocket a picture of his mother or a locket of her hair.[13]

The [Roman Catholic] Church changed the observance of the Sab-bath to Sunday by right of the divine, infallible authority given to her by her founder, Jesus Christ. The Protestant claiming the Bible to be the only guide of faith, has no warrant for observing Sunday.[14]

For more documentation about the rise of the Roman Catholic Church, and for abundant proof that Reformation Protestants like Martin Luther, John Calvin, John Wesley, and Charles Spurgeon identified the Roman Church as the "little horn" (see Daniel 7:8), "the beast" (Revelation 13:1), and "Mys-tery, Babylon" (see Revelation 17:5), see Steve Wohlberg's book, *End Time*

Delusions: The Rapture, the Antichrist, Israel, and the End of the World. Available from White Horse Media, 1-800-78-BIBLE.

MORE FASCINATING BOOKS BY STEVE WOHLBERG
Pocketbooks:
> *The United States in Bible Prophecy*
> *Rapture Myths*
> *Solving the Mystery of Death*
> *Perils of Talking to the Dead*
> *The Millennium*
> *The Hot Topic of Hell*
> *The End of the World: Fact Versus Fiction*
> *Discovering the Lost Sabbath Truth*
> *Decoding the Mark of the Beast*
> *Perils of Harry Potter and Witchcraft*
> *The Darkness of Twilight*
> *Surviving Toxic Terrorism*
> *Fabulous Health Made Simple*
> *Juice Your Way to Fabulous Health*

Books:
> *Truth Left Behind*
> *From Hollywood to Heaven: The Steve Wohlberg Story*
> *End Time Delusions: The Rapture, the Antichrist, Israel, and the End of the World*
> *Demons in Disguise: The Danger of Talking to the Dead*
> *The Trouble with Twilight*
> *Exposing Harry Potter and Witchcraft*
> *Will My Pet Go to Heaven?*
> *The Character of God Controversy*

Available from White Horse Media
1-800-782-4253
www.whitehorsemedia.com

To sign up for Steve Wohlberg's free e-mail newsletter, for information on how to watch White Horse Media's television programs, or to view many other eye-opening books, tracts, and DVDs, visit www.whitehorsemedia.com. You can also "Like" Steve on www.facebook.com/stevewohlberg or "Follow" him on Twitter @WhiteHorse7.

1. *Webster's Dictionary,* 1929 edition.

2. *Mosheim's Ecclesiastical History,* century ii, part ii, ch. iv, par. 7.

3. Schaff-Herzog *Encyclopedia of Religious Knowledge,* Art. "Sunday."

4. From the Early Church Father, St. Justin. Quoted in the *New Official Catholic Catechism* (1994), 524.

5. *Code of Justinian,* book 3, title 12, law 3.

6. Ch. xx, par. 3.

7. Arthur P. Stanley, *History of the Eastern Church,* lect. vi, par. 14.

8. Ibid., 184; emphasis supplied.

9. Henry Milman, *The History of Christianity,* book 2, chap. 8, vol. 22, 175.

10. Socrates Scholasticus, *Ecclesiastical History,* book 5, ch. 22.

11. Sozomen, *Ecclesiastical History,* book 7, ch. 19.

12. Rev. Peter Geiermann C.S.S.R., *The Convert's Catechism of Catholic Doctrine,* 50.

13. Rev. John O' Brien, *The Faith of Millions: The Credentials of the Catholic Religion,* 473.

14. The Catholic Universe Bulletin, August 14, 1942, 4.